Tasting Kaua'i
Restaurants

by Marta Lane

Tasting Kaua'i: Restaurants

An Insider's Guide to Eating Well on the Garden Island

Copyright © 2016 by Marta Lane & Tasting Kaua'i LLC.

Edited by Hiyaguha Cohen and Coco Zickos

Cover, design and photography by Daniel Lane of www.PonoPhoto.com

Information offered in this book is based on the author's preferences refined by research as a Kaua'i-based food and farm writer. We offer no guarantees and assume the reader understands that fluctuations in quality occur. This book is updated annually and cannot accommodate menu changes between editions.

Text is Times New Roman font

ISBN-10: 0989448614

ISBN-13: 978-0-9894486-1-1

For more information, visit www.TastingKauai.com

Printed in U.S.A

About the cover

Front Cover clockwise from top: 1. Sunset view over the Kalalau Valley. 2. Seared 'ahi at Nalu Kai Grill & Bar. 3. Scallops at the Kaua'i Grill. 4. Chefs flambé at Makana Terrace. 5. Da Bruddah Burger at the North Shore General Store. 6. Spicy pork chop at RumFire Po'ipū Beach.

Back Cover left to right: 1. Ox Tail Soup at MCS Grill. 2. Sunset at Nalu Kai. 3. A smoked Rum-Hattan at RumFire Po'ipū Beach.

In Good Company

I am eternally grateful to my husband, Daniel Lane, for his support and patience, which have allowed me to grow into myself. His devotion to detail and creative spirit have brought this book to life and ushered my dream into reality.

I am fortunate to do work that matters to me by connecting the dots and tracing how food gets to our communal table.

Thank you to Kaua'i's farmers and chefs who have guided me through their fields and kitchens, all the while answering countless questions.

Thank you, Jillian Seals, for teaching me how to grow food; Dave Power, for always saying yes; Ron Miller, for letting me know my work makes a difference; Guy Higa for your willingness to experiment and promote local food; and Jean-Marie Josselin, for your unwavering support.

I have enormous gratitude for my mentor, Pamela Varma Brown, whose high vibration and generous spirit have encouraged and informed me.

A heartfelt mahalo goes to Dania Katz, Jeanne Toulon, Nalani Brun, Stephanie Donoho and Sue Kanoho for sage advice and gentle guidance. Imua!

I appreciate the support of my readers and our community, as well as our talented Tasting Kaua'i team including Michelle Lemay (director of food tours), Monique Tucker (sales and marketing) and Tiana Laranio (ambassador of aloha and back-up tour guide).

I wouldn't have the courage to be who I am if it weren't for Bruce and Magda Armstrong, my parents, who wed in 1954 and are still alive and well, living in Colorado.

Judy Armstrong, Ilissa Moregon and Julie Cobb, your love and light lift me to the sky. I am immensely grateful to be alive and thriving on this beautiful island. Mahalo ke Akua for that!

"One cannot think well,
love well, sleep well,
if one has not dined well."

Virginia Woolf

TABLE OF CONTENTS

SOUTH SHORE

WEST SIDE

ADDITIONAL INFORMATION

INTRODUCTION

When I travel, I like to drench myself in the sights, sounds, smells and tastes of the area. I submit to local customs and crave regional food. After all, food defines a destination and connects people to the land and its cultural history. On my first trip to Kaua'i, I longed for a book to help me plan a vacation steeped in local food. This is that book.

Written by a foodie for foodies, *Tasting Kaua'i: Restaurants* is an exclusive listing based on insider information. Since 2010, I have been writing professionally about the best farmers, produce, chefs, restaurants and food artisans on Kaua'i. My husband, Daniel, is a professional photographer who works by my side. We've toured more than 90 farms and countless restaurant kitchens, while learning about the work that goes into the food we eat.

I write about humble diners and food trucks that make fresh, affordable meals as well as tapas bars, swanky lounges and elite restaurants with sweeping views. As a full-time food writer, many people think of me as a food critic. But I like to call myself a food profiler. Instead of focusing on what's wrong, I choose to focus on what's right.

I am a foodie at heart and read cookbooks for fun. I've been on food tours in the Rockies and learned how to make bread at Whole Foods through a workshop by Slow Food Denver. I'm a certified personal chef, a graduate of a 12-week organic farming course and a certified Hawai'i Master Food Preserver. Our Kaua'i Food Tours are edible experiences designed for foodies like me, who want to connect deeply with the people and tastes of Kaua'i.

I'm an advocate for food that's grown in a way that benefits everything on this planet. Not just the people who eat it, but the people who grow and harvest it. I also care about how farms affect the land, water and air as well as the wildlife that thrives in ecosystems created within diversified farms.

When restaurants list local products on their menus, it means we eat food that's extremely fresh and, therefore, more flavorful. It also supports our small community and reduces the island's carbon footprint.

The Garden Island is home to a lot of passionate cooks who make really good food. While Kaua'i's food can't be compared to New York or Spain, our little paradise holds its own. It is my hope that people, who support what we do, combined with the restaurants listed in our book, will bolster food security on Kaua'i.

After our first edition was released, residents told me they left our guidebook in their car for easy reference while running errands. Returning visitors said they used it daily and it never let them down. A Hawai'i health educator even called to thank me for making healthy food options easy to find. Our "Tasting Kaua'i" app, which can be downloaded to smartphones and tables, makes it even easier to eat well on Kaua'i!

In essence, this book is about real food. Real. Fresh. Food.

If you're the kind of person who prefers making macaroni and cheese from scratch instead of grabbing a box off the shelf, then this is the book for you. If you prefer unique and sometimes funky environments, where the creativity of the chef spills into the dining area, then this is the book for you. If you're partial to the predictability of chain restaurants, I hear they're opening a national steak house on Kaua'i soon. But don't look for it in this book!

*Marta Lane harvests taro with Adam Asquith of Kealia Farm
and Maris Manzano, owner of Verde*

HOW WE CHOOSE RESTAURANTS

A passion for promoting wholesome food drives me. Not a single restaurant has paid us to be in our book, blog or app.

When deciding whom to list, we go by taste. I may see a new place while driving, or a reader, chef or friend may recommend something. Daniel and I try it out as regular customers. If we like what we eat, I call them up and schedule an interview.

When we arrive, I talk story with the chef and learn how their food is made. Many people are intimidated when being interviewed, but since I'm there to celebrate food, they quickly become comfortable and their passion soon spills into the conversation.

I learn how they got into the business and why cooking makes them happy. I learn about their struggles and triumphs. I get a copy of the menu and go over it with the chef. French fries that took three days to make; house-cured bacon; nourishing meals made from whole, locally raised animals; smoked meat; whole, local fish cut just before it's cooked; house-baked bread; fresh vegetables bought at the farmers market; house-made mustards, pickles and sauces and handcrafted cocktails—all these are just some of the things restaurants do here every day.

When I first started, I couldn't believe I was getting paid to write about food! As it turns out, it's a lot like work. I've learned that I take good food seriously. During a meal I take copious notes of how things taste, look, smell, feel and even sound. I notice the atmosphere, if the energy is convivial and how clean the place is.

If we like a restaurant, it's featured on our blog. Our favorites are listed in our restaurant guidebook and app. If we really like a restaurant, a pink hibiscus identifies it. Making food with fresh ingredients and sourcing locally takes a lot of extra time and effort, and we highlight those who make that a priority.

HAWAI'I FOOD BANK — KAUA'I BANCH

Daniel and I are very fortunate to have our kitchen stocked with healthy, vibrant food grown and made on Kaua'i. We realize that not everyone is as lucky. With a strong desire to make fresh food available to everyone, we donate a portion of the proceeds from the sale of all books and Kaua'i Food Tours to the Hawai'i Food Bank—Kaua'i Branch. Mahalo nui loa (thank you very much) for all the work you do to keep our island's children, women and men fed.

HOW TO USE THIS BOOK

While there are nearly 700 restaurants on Kaua'i, this collection is an exclusive listing based on our work. I describe food that I have tasted so you can get an idea of the type of food served at each location.

Our book gets updated every year, but restaurants change their menus more often than that. Don't be dismayed if you go to a restaurant and they no longer serve a dish that's featured here. Order what looks good. I'm sure you'll enjoy it! Restaurant hours also change. For these reasons, our e-book and print editions include a link to each restaurant's website or Facebook page so you can find current menus and hours.

Restaurants that have closed are listed at the bottom of the "Kaua'i Restaurant Guide" page on our website.

Our guidebook is also available as an app, which includes hours of operation, nearby restaurants and searchable icons (see "Understanding the Icons" in the next section). Download the app form smartphones and tablets at app.tastingkauai.com.

This book also includes the address, phone number and type of food served (i.e.: Hawai'i Regional Cuisine, Mexican, etc.)

Some "restaurants" are only at farmers markets. For a complete listing of farmers markets, visit www.TastingKauai.com and click on the "Farmers Market" tab. If you're new to Hawai'i, you may be apprehensive about eating exotic produce. I guide a farmers market tour, which includes tastings and introductions to farmers, and have found this empowers people to cook with locally grown ingredients.

The information offered in this book is based on my preferences, which are refined by research as a Kaua'i-based food and farm writer. I offer no guarantees and assume the reader understands that fluctuations in quality may occur.

Listings are divided into five zones: North Shore, East Side, Central, South Shore and West Side. Icons identify food service and dress code at a glance. We assume that each of the modern, tourist-friendly restaurants follows this broad set of procedures:

1. Accepts major credit cards

2. Has an up-to-date website

3. Is kid-friendly

FOOD SERVICE

These abbreviations indicate the types of meals each establishment serves.

BREAKFAST

LUNCH

DINNER

 COCKTAILS

This means the location has a bar where you can hang out and have a drinks.

 DESSERTS

This lets you know the establishment specializes in something tasty for after dinner, or any time you need a sweet treat.

PRICE RANGE

This represents an average price range. Some entrées may be more or less. If any combination of breakfast, lunch or dinner is served, the price range represents the dinner menu. One dollar sign indicates most entrées range between $5 and $10. Two dollar signs represent entrées that average $10 to $20. Three dollar signs indicate a menu where most entrées are $20 and above. Prices listed are based on the time of this printing; they may, of course, change.

SLIPPAH CODE

"Hang Loose" is not only a saying but a lifestyle, and in Hawai'i, most everyone walks around in flip-flop sandals known as slippahs. I've decided to honor this casual island tradition with a dignified place in my listings. The Slippah Code is a simple system that ranks a restaurant's dress code. There are three general categories, because in paradise we don't like to get too complicated!

ONE SLIPPAH

Very casual. You can go dressed in a bikini top and sarong, because your only options are to eat outside or take it with you.

TWO SLIPPAH

You better put on a T-shirt, and make sure you have both slippahs on your feet. If you've been playing in the water, bring a dry towel to sit on because salt water damages the chairs. Once you have satisfied these minimum requirements, anything else is a bonus.

THREE SLIPPAH

Wash off the salt water and put on your finest aloha wear. Wear nice shoes, linen pants or a flouncy dress. You could certainly get buttoned up for these fine-dining restaurants, but why? We're in paradise!

RESERVATIONS

 If you see this icon, that means reservations are recommended.

ALTERNATIVE DIETS

Kauaʻi is a haven for those seeking healthy lifestyles and food options. Most of the restaurants listed have menu items or substitutions for those on alternative diets.

VEGETARIAN

 This Leaf icon illustrates which restaurants offer vegetarian meals that are more than salads. For this listing, the definition of vegetarian includes dairy products and eggs, but no fish or animal meat.

VEGAN

 This icon indicates that a restaurant offers vegans more options than just salads.

GLUTEN-FREE

 This GF icon marks which restaurants offer gluten-free options, but be aware that meals are not necessarily made in a dedicated gluten-free environment.

WI-FI

 This icon indicates free Wi-Fi is available.

FOOD TRUCK

 Kauaʻi has some amazing food trucks that serve fresh, flavorful meals quickly. Some folks are nervous about eating at food trucks, but you won't be disappointed when eating at these. Food trucks are my go-to when I want fast food.

FARMERS MARKET

 A lot of local food businesses start out by selling their products at the Island's farmers markets. We have listed a few as well as the specific farmers market(s) at which these chefs sell. Some of these people are available as private chefs and offer catering services as well. We have included a short list of private chefs at the end of this book.

SPECIAL ICONS

FAVORITES

People often ask which restaurant on Kaua'i is my favorite. The question is always presented in a conspiratorial tone that suggests, "If you could only eat at one place, where would it be?" It's a tough question because there are too many considerations for a blanket, one-size-fits-all answer. It depends on what kind of ambiance I'm in the mood for, how hungry I am, how much time and money I want to spend, what side of the island I'm on and the kind of food I'm craving. You can be sure that if you see this icon, the listing is one of our top considerations!

HAWAI'I REGIONAL CUISINE

In 1935, Pan American Airways began to fly visitors to Hawai'i. At the time, Hawai'i's high-end restaurants were only located in resorts, and European chefs cooked ingredients, which were flown in from across the world. In the early 1980s, 12 chefs came together to figure out how they could source fresh ingredients—especially fish—locally. By using diverse ethnic techniques when cooking local ingredients, these chefs created Hawai'i Regional Cuisine. The movement provided local growers with an expanding market, and forever changed food in Hawai'i. Today, many restaurants serve Hawai'i Regional Cuisine–but in this book, this icon means the restaurant is owned and/or operated by a founding HRC chef. Those chefs include:

1. Sam Choy
2. Roger Dikon
3. Mark Ellman
4. Amy Ferguson
5. Bev Gannon
6. Jean-Marie Josselin
7. George "Mavro" Mavrothalassitis
8. Peter Merriman
9. Philippe Padovani
10. Gary Strehl
11. Alan Wong
12. Roy Yamaguchi

HAWAIIAN LANGUAGE

Navigating Kaua'i is a lot more fun when you have basic language skills. I've included a short summary of Hawaiian language rules, its alphabet and commonly mispronounced words on the Garden Island. Learning to pronounce each vowel, and perfecting your glottal stop, will enable you to be clearly understood should you have to ask for directions. Plus, it's fun!

RULES

- There are no consonant clusters in the Hawaiian language.

- Hawaiian words end with a vowel.

- All Hawaiian words have at least one vowel.

- An 'okina (') is a glottal stop. It is considered a consonant, and only appears between vowels.

- The kahakō (¯) makes vowels longer, so it only occurs over vowels.

HAWAIIAN ALPHABET

There are 13 letters in the Hawaiian alphabet: a, e, h, i, k, l, m, n, o, p, u, w and the 'okina. Consonants are pronounced the same as they are in English, and the 'okina (') is the sound that occurs between "oh-oh." The vowels—stressed and unstressed—sound like:

a - "ah," like the a in above

ā - "aah," like the a in avocado

e - "eh," like the e in let

ē - "ayy," like the e in net

i - "ee," like the e in easy

ī - "eee," like the ee in bee

o - "oh," like the o in pole

ō - "ohh," like the o in goal

u - "oo," like the u in tune

ū - "ooo," like the oo in moon

Vowel combinations are usually merged into a single sound. For example ou, as in soul; oi, as in loiter; au, like "ow" in pow; ae, like "y" in my; ei, as in veil; ai, like "i" in like; au, like "ou" in out; and au, like "ow" in low.

PLURAL

There is no "s" in the Hawaiian language. The basic way to pluralize a word is to put "nā" before the word. For example: lei, neck garland; nā lei, neck garlands. Pua, flower; nā pua, flowers.

MISPRONOUNCED WORDS

This is a general guideline when pronouncing popular streets, destinations and cities. A space represents the 'okina, or glottal stop, and a dash indicates the pronunciation within one group of letters. Often, the 'okina is removed but I have included it here.

WORD	PRONUNCIATION
Kaua'i	Kah-wa e
Kōke'e	Ko-keh eh
'Ele'ele	El-eh el-eh
Po'ipū	Po ee-poo
Līhu'e	Lee-hoo eh
Nāwiliwili	Na-wee-lee-wee-lee
Kapa'a	Kah-pah ah
Hā'ena	Hah ay-nah
Ke'e	Keh eh
Wai'ale'ale	Why ah-lay ah-lay
Maha'ulepu	Ma-ha oo-lay-poo
Opaeka'a	Oh-pie-kah ah
Kuamo'o	Ku-ah-mo oh
Kūhiō	Koo-he-oh

A sampling of the day's fresh catch of menpachi

NORTH SHORE

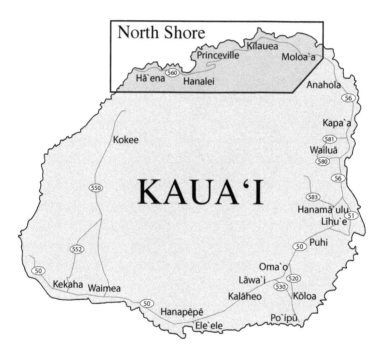

Waves crashing at sunset along the Na Pali Coast

AKAMAI JUICE CO.

5-5134 Kūhiō Hwy., Hanalei
www.AkamaiJuice.com
808-639-3513
Fresh Juice, Raw Vegan Food

Akamai Juice Co. prepares fresh fruit juices and raw vegan food, which are delivered to homes and vacation rentals along the North Shore. On weekday mornings, owner Cas Schwabe can be found at Tahiti Nui serving her drinkable health potions that were inspired while catering for movie stars on Hollywood sets.

"Heavy hitters like Martin Scorcese need to be on in the morning," she says. "I'd tell him, 'I know you don't like anything heavy, so with your grapefruit sections, try this.' And it would resonate with him; it would light him up a little bit. It turned him on to another side of nutrition."

The Super Green has a day's worth of vitamins and minerals in one glass. Akamai Bop, her diabetic and Atkins friendly drink, is made with apple banana, orange juice and pineapple. Chicoban contains chico sapote, apple bananas, macadamia nuts, honey, organic almond milk and ice. Keiki Love is loaded with apple banana, papaya, pineapple, passion fruit, lime and honey.

While on the set for HBO's mini-series *True Detective*, Cas learned the intricacies of a raw, vegan diet while cooking for Matthew McConaughey and Woody Harrelson, the show's detectives.

"Woody's been a strict organic raw vegan for 23-years," Schwabe explains. "He really helped me hone raw vegan cheffing and he tells people that I'm one of the top three in the world."

One of those people he told was McConaughey, who was born and raised in Texas and ate meat at every meal. By the end of production, Cas says he was on a gluten-free, raw vegan diet and stealing Harrelson's meals.

"I brought Woody's food into his bus and Matthew was there," recalls Schwabe. "He took a bite of zucchini fries, and his eyes opened wide, he smiled, wagged his eyebrows and said, 'Try these Matthew, they're off the richter! And this barbecued tahini ketchup is crazy!' Matthew tried it, along with my Falafel Dagwood sandwich, and literally walked off the bus with Woody's plate of food!"

Cas Schwabe at the Hanalei Farmers Market

18

BarAcuda

Hanalei Center
5-5161 Kūhiō Hwy., Hanalei
808-826-7081
www.RestaurantBarAcuda.com
Mediterranean-style Tapas

Bar Acuda owner Jim Moffat learned from his parents how communal meals could enrich life. This lesson was especially poignant when he was 11 years old and his family vacationed in the Bahamas.

"One evening my dad handed us a huge net and sent us off down the pier to catch crabs. We boiled up a big pot of water and put all these huge crabs in it and we just sat there and tore them open," recalls Moffat, who in 1996, was listed as one of America's 10 best new chefs in *Food & Wine* magazine.

Today, his trendy tapas bar, which is located in the heart of Hanalei, generates a convivial atmosphere where diners linger over food and drinks. Candlelight glints off silver chrome in the open kitchen while diners sit at rustic tables dressed with fine tableware. Outside, a view of the North Shore's majestic peaks cocoon diners who sit along a lanai that runs the length of the restaurant.

BarAcuda's menu changes seasonally and includes small and large plates. Menu items have included oven-roasted local "head on" spot prawns and South Pacific shrimp with garlic and smoky paprika sauce; ali'i mushrooms and little potatoes roasted in parchment paper with garlic, wine, butter and herbs; grilled all-natural Angus flank steak with pommes frites; and a chocolate pot de creme with coconut macaroon and whipped cream.

Jim cultivated his food philosophy after traveling to Italy, Southern France, Spain and Portugal, then cooking in San Francisco for more than 25 years at his award-winning restaurants. Today, his passion for sustainable agriculture is fostered by direct relationships with local farmers, fishermen and ranchers.

"The beautiful thing about food is that it forces communication and family," says Moffat. "It's an excuse for connection."

LAULAU LOVE

IF YOU'RE TRYING LAULAU FOR THE FIRST TIME, WE RECOMMEND HANALEI TARO & JUICE CO. THAT'S BECAUSE WE WANT TO SET THE BAR HIGH FOR YOU. THEIR KĀLUA PORK LAULAU IS FANTASTIC, BUT IF YOU WANT A LOWER CALORIE OPTION, GET THE CHICKEN LAULAU. JUST KNOW THAT IT'S PREPARED WITH BONE-IN THIGHS. (FOR A COMPLETE DESCRIPTION, SEE THE GLOSSARY ON PAGE 144)

VEGAN

At The Bistro, chef de cuisine, John Paul Gordon, focuses on using fresh and local ingredients to create European classics with a decidedly Pacific taste. Gordon brings in fresh fish, Kaua'i Shrimp, produce from about 10 North Shore farmers and grass-fed beef from the West Side.

Popular Fish Rockets are cigar-sized pieces of 'ahi seasoned with furikake, wrapped in lumpia and flash-fried. They are drizzled with wasabi aioli and herb oil and served over coleslaw made with locally grown Napa cabbage and fat shreds of local carrots all tossed in a house-made dressing.

"They're so good, I have to keep them on the menu," says Gordon. "I took them off once and had an uprising with our regular customers."

Curly Kale Salad includes raw kale "massaged" with truffle oil and lemon juice and topped with slivered almonds and creamy Kaua'i Kunana Dairy goat cheese.

"Kale is very fibrous," explains Gordon, "so we lomi it, which is massage in Hawaiian, to break it down. The lemon juice helps to do that as well."

Prosciutto & Goat is an addicting combination of prosciutto stuffed with local goat cheese. Smoky, salty and meaty flavors melt into creamy cheese and then magic happens when sweet honey, crunchy walnuts and tart raisins join the culinary chorus.

The St. Louis BBQ Ribs take three days to make and won "People's Choice" and "Best in Meat" at the 2015 Taste of Hawai'i. Gordon starts by rubbing the ribs in dry spices and letting them marinate for two days. The ribs are braised, cooled then grilled with homemade barbecue sauce and served with that terrific coleslaw.

There are 120 varieties of wine, a handful of martinis and six handcrafted cocktails. We appreciated the strength of the mai tai, made with light rum, house-made juice mix, guava puree and dark rum. Coconut Cactus is a refreshing blend of Espolon tequila, coconut water, ginger and fresh lime juice.

St. Louis Barbecue Ribs with house-made BBQ sauce and coleslaw

Tip: Takeout containers are banned from the restaurant to foster a lighter environmental impact on our beautiful island. That means no cups, no containers and no plastic forks or knives.

THE DOLPHIN

5-5016 Kūhiō Hwy., Hanalei
808-826-6113
www.HanaleiDolphin.com
Fresh Fish and Sushi

For more than 30-years, the Dolphin restaurant, fish market and sushi bar in Hanalei has cultivated solid relationships with a handful of local fishermen and according to Bryson Sugahara, working with Kaua'i-based fishermen means better quality

"The Dolphin restaurant is unique because every three days we get whole fish straight from Kaua'i's waters," says Sugahara, general manager of the Dolphin restaurants in Hanalei and Po'ipū.

With two restaurants, two sushi bars and two fish markets, the Dolphin goes through roughly 1,500 pounds of fresh local fish every week. On a typical day, there can be whole ono, 'ahi, opah and monchong hanging in the cooler.

"If you buy from the [Honolulu] auction, the fish goes through eight hands before it gets to the plate," Sugahara explains. "You got the long-liner fisherman, the person who delivers to the auction block, the auction block cuts and displays the fish, there's a packing guy and then it has to be shipped. Finally, the local distributor gets it and delivers it to the restaurant. At the Dolphin, it only goes through two hands."

Both North and South Shore menus are the same and include the Po'ipū Roll. Diced Japanese hamachi is lightly tossed with house-made sriracha aioli and wrapped in shiso—a pungent Japanese herb that tastes like basil and mint. A tempura asparagus spear is tucked alongside and the roll is topped with seasonal fish.

The Dolphin specializes in fusion sushi, which combines global cuisines and creates original, tasty rolls. The sushi bar offers omakase, or chef's choice, where guests are asked what they like and the sushi chef creates it for them.

Rainbow Poke with radish sprouts at The Dolphin

An 8-ounce 'ahi steak is marinated for more than 24 hours in the Dolphin's signature Teriyaki 'Ahi. A bath in the light, brothy teriyaki sauce infuses the meaty tuna with a subtle flavor. It's delightful on its own, but the Dolphin serves it with a side of melted butter, which adds rich succulence.

If the staff isn't busy, ask them to take you into the walk-in cooler and check out the fresh fish that's hanging. You'll be shocked and awed!

HANALEI BREAD CO.

Hanalei Town Center
5-5161 Kūhiō Hwy. #4, Hanalei
808-826-7081
www.restaurantbaracuda.com/hanalei-bread-shop
Bakery

Inside Hanalei Bread Co., apple and walnut scones, croissants and Danishes filled with house-made jam line the front counter. Behind the cash register, piles of fresh baked bread are loaded into wicker baskets. At the hot counter, fresh egg dishes such as gluten-free crepes, or baked eggs with tomatoes and ricotta, as well as breakfast pizza and sandwiches are made to order. Beverages include espresso made with locally grown and roasted beans, Maui cold-press coffee; fresh-pressed juice, smoothies and tropical fruit spritzers. All of the grains and nuts that are used to make about 14 types of rustic, country style bread are organic and so is the dairy. The bakery uses Kauaʻi honey and a North Shore farmer delivers 1000 eggs twice a week.

Dine and enjoy a view of Hanalei

Hanalei Roasters formerly occupied the building that was built in 1906. Today, they roast Hawaiʻi grown coffee beans in Līhuʻe and supply the bakery. Jim Moffat sold Living Foods Market & Cafe, a gourmet grocery store in Poʻipū, in the spring of 2014. The South Shore market had a bakery that Jim missed, so he opened Hanalei Bread Co. in Dec. 2015.

"The climate on the North Shore is different, so we had to change all of the recipes," Moffat says. "Making bread is so rudimentary. Combine flour, water, yeast and salt and from there you can make hundreds of different breads."

When Jim took over, massive renovations were made and six dumpsters were filled. Today, the space is accessible, uncluttered and exposed to the outdoors. Fresh pastries and bread are baked every night and in the morning, massive doors made of Brazilian sapele wood slide open, turning the bakery into a cafe. Countertop tables with bench seats line the edge of the cafe so diners can people watch.

"My father had a boathouse with doors like these," Moffat says, running his hands along the smooth, thick wood. "The place used to be uncomfortably crowded and there was nowhere to go after you ordered. Now, people can sit on the deck and watch Hanalei, which is very colorful."

HANALEI TARO & JUICE CO.

5-5070 Kūhiō Hwy., Hanalei
808-826-1059
www.HanaleiTaro.com
Traditional Hawaiian Food with a Modern Twist

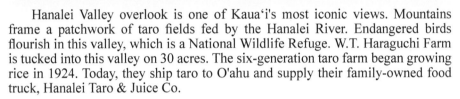

Hanalei Valley overlook is one of Kaua'i's most iconic views. Mountains frame a patchwork of taro fields fed by the Hanalei River. Endangered birds flourish in this valley, which is a National Wildlife Refuge. W.T. Haraguchi Farm is tucked into this valley on 30 acres. The six-generation taro farm began growing rice in 1924. Today, they ship taro to O'ahu and supply their family-owned food truck, Hanalei Taro & Juice Co.

"We are a farm-to-fork taro shop that makes authentic Hawaiian food with a contemporary twist," says cook and owner Brad Nakayama.

Taro is slipped into almost everything. Fresh poi is hand-made three times a week. There are 16 varieties of taro smoothies, taro mochi and an açaí bowl with taro granola. There's even an addicting taro hummus and a nutrient-packed taro burger.

Brad's wife, Lyndsey Haraguchi-Nakayama, grew up sampling her mother's taro recipes in the family kitchen. The best were passed on to Brad and he uses them today. For example, he transforms whole hogs from Kaneshiro Farm in Oma'o into kālua pig that is moist, rich, salty and smoky.

That pork, along with taro and poi, shows up throughout the small menu. The Kālua Pig Plate, served in a biodegradable container, comes with sweet poi (or rice), taro mac salad, lomi salmon and kūlolo, a traditional Hawaiian dessert made with taro and coconut.

The laulau's thick layer of taro leaves encloses chicken or pork. When you remove a strip of inedible ti leaf that holds the bundle tight, your fork pierces a pudgy layer of rich greens and slides through tender meat.

Brad makes a special every day. Past specials have included shoyu chicken, kālua turkey with taro stuffing and lomi pineapple, Okinawan pork belly sliders with Asian slaw on taro buns, Portuguese taro soup and local lamb curry with taro.

Hanalei Taro & Juice Co.'s Zesty Taro Hummus and Hanalei Taro Veggie Burgers are available at Sueoka Store, Westin Princeville and Menehune Marts in Kapahi and Kīlauea. Their food truck is also parked at the Kaua'i Community Market on Saturdays at Kaua'i Community College and every Wednesday during lunch at Born Hawai'i, a store in downtown in Kapa'a.

Brad Nakayama and Lyndsey Haraguchi-Nakayama

KAUA'I GRILL

St. Regis Princeville Resort
5520 Ka Haku Road, Princeville
808-826-9644
www.KauaiGrill.com
Hawai'i Regional Cuisine

Mount Makana finishes out the curve of Hanalei Bay, its majestic peak the signature statement at the end of the North Shore's mountain range. Along the horizon, a small sailboat rides a southbound drift. In the distance, a cruise ship creeps across a Pacific Ocean that looks like blue silk flowing on a lazy breeze. It's hard to pull my eyes from the panoramic view, which is one of 20 listed on *Food & Wine* magazine's online article "World's Best Restaurant Views."

Inside, lovers cuddle in the curve of plush booths. They gaze from giant windows, laugh and sip champagne. Faces glow in the glory of a sunset that turns the sky into an inferno of red and orange. Contemporary music plays just under party level.

Kaua'i Grill's menu is seasonal and items have included a gorgeous appetizer made with ruby red slices of kampachi from Hawai'i Island that's cured in sugar, salt and beet juice, alternate with juicy orange segments. Pan roasted onaga includes a generous portion of buttery white fish (skin fried to a perfect crisp) and roasted cherry tomatoes, summer squash, wax beans and a drizzle of fruity extra virgin olive oil.

Grilled Makaweli Tenderloin is made with grass-fed cattle that are raised and processed on Kaua'i's west side. Seared on the outside, there's a bit of crisp crust that encloses the interior's juicy flesh. The deeply flavorful filet is topped with Hamakua mushrooms and a soy caramel emulsion. When combined, all three turn the umami (savory) factor up to ten. It's a powerful sonnet to meat lovers and what I think of when I imagine the taste of beef.

Pan seared scallops are surrounded by a luscious pool of champagne and thyme butter sauce with nubs of roasted corn and crisply rendered Portuguese sausage. Soft-cooked Kaua'i quail eggs are placed on top of two plump scallops and popcorn tossed in a spicy blend adds a playful crunch. If there was a dish that represented the opulence and whimsy of the St. Regis Princeville, this would be it.

Fresh Hawaii-grown heart of palm salad

KAUA'I JUICE CO.

4270 Kīlauea Rd, Kīlauea
808-634-0886
www.KauaiJuiceCo.com
Cold-Pressed Juice Bar

The Kaua'i Juice Co. has three locations on the island, but their main one is located in Kapa'a. If you turn to page 59, you can read the complete description.

Kaua'i Juice Co. offers a rainbow of flavor

SEASIDE TAPAS

NALI KAI IS A HIDDEN GEM THAT ONLY SERVES TAPAS FROM MAY THROUGH SEPTEMBER, AND AGAIN IN DECEMBER. OTHERWISE, THE MENU FEATURES COCKTAILS AND A POOLSIDE LUNCH. EITHER WAY, THE RESORT PROVIDES COMPLIMENTARY VALET PARKING AND EVERY RESTAURANT IS OPEN TO THE PUBLIC.

When I spoke with Justin Smith, owner of Kaua'i Ono, about 40 people were sitting down for dinner as the sun set over the North Shore. The "FarmFishForage" meal was held on a grassy lawn and guests sat on benches at wide wood tables made from reclaimed pallets. Votive candles flickered in mason jars set on bare tabletops, which were arranged under a white canopy strung with twinkle lights.

As he cooked inside his gleaming, stainless steel mobile kitchen, black-clad waiters made sure everyone was seated for one of the pop-up dinners that is held three times a week. We had no idea what was coming, but our anticipation was quenched with sips of wine that we brought from home.

Justin forages for fruit growing wild on Kaua'i's mountainsides. He doesn't cook with wheat, flour or beans, or showcase anything that didn't grow on Kaua'i. For him, it's not about "local," "gluten-free," or "free-range"; he sees edible opportunities everywhere.

"I believe in using what we have available," he says. "Why a single banana is ever imported to this island blows my mind. My events are about being resourceful and changing the perspective of what can be done with what is right in front of us."

The Kauai Ono breadfruit croquette with braised local beef and a zesty caper sauce

Justin Smith of Kauaʻi Ono after one of his popular farm-to-table dinners

After traveling through Latin America and Mexico, Justin attended culinary school in San Sebastián, a resort town on the Northwest coast of Spain, and cooked at Arzak, an award-winning restaurant owned by Juan Mari Arzak that's famous for New Basque Cuisine.

"I spent nine months in his restaurant," recalls Smith. "At the time, he was ranked third in the world."

The evening's five-course dinner began with organic steamed taro root topped with steamed taro leaves and drizzled with coconut sauce. We also had Kīlauea greens with sesame ginger vinaigrette; brined and smoked walu (escolar) with olive oil rubbed kale; breadfruit croquettes topped with braised local beef and caper sauce; and a flourless chocolate torte with kumquat marmalade.

By the end of the meal, boisterous conversation punctuated by peals of laughter transformed strangers into friends.

"I never planned on doing really amazing food," Justin says above the din of merriment. "It's just food that is super clean and very simple."

BALI HAʻI

THE HANALEI VALLEY IS SURROUNDED BY FIVE VERDANT MOUNTAINS, ONE OF WHICH IS MOUNT MAKANA. THE 1,115-FOOT MOUNTAIN WAS FEATURED IN THE 1958 FILM ADAPTATION OF THE MUSICAL SOUTH PACIFIC AS BALI HAʻI, A NAME THAT IS STILL USED TODAY.

KĪLAUEA BAKERY & PAU HANA PIZZA

2484 Keneke St., Kīlauea
808-828-2020
www.KilaueaBakery.com
Bakery and Pizza

Since 1990, Kīlauea Bakery & Pau Hana Pizza has established itself as a reliable source of baked goods and savory, wholesome meals. Owner Thomas Pickett, originally from the San Francisco Bay Area, graduated from the Culinary Institute of America in Hyde Park, New York, in 1981. He, along with wife and business manager Katie, moved to Kaua'i in 1985 when the couple transferred from the Sheraton Waikoloa on Hawai'i Island.

Today, the bakery uses a sourdough starter that Tom made in 1986 while working as a pastry chef at the Sheraton Princeville. Days begin at 4 a.m., when loaves of bread are popped into the oven after proofing for 18 hours.

"Our Molasses Rye is always mentioned when Kīlauea is mentioned," Tom tells me as we share lunch under an umbrella at one of the bakery's outside tables. Defying my image of a baker, his blue eyes shine as he feeds his lean frame with massive slices of fresh-baked pizza.

Tom's team also prepares 40 different pastries, including New York style bagels, Polish bialys (like hole-less bagels with savory fillings), dark chocolate dipped guava macaroons and éclairs filled with pastry cream that is made from local coconuts.

Thomas Pickett, Owner of Kilauea Bakery & Pau Hana Pizza

Frustrated with the cost and landfill waste of canned coconut milk, Tom invented and patented a "coconut faucet," and a friend built "Vlad the Impaler." About 50 pounds of North Shore coconuts are drained using Tom's faucet before they're cracked open on Vlad. Three pounds of coconut meat are harvested, whipped into pastry cream and loaded into éclairs, which are draped with dark chocolate.

Next to Vlad is a noni press, which Tom created to make Tom's Super Sonic Noni Tonic. Similar to a cider press, ripe noni is pressed and a clear juice is collected. Ginger, turmeric and Hawaiian chili pepper juice is added to soften noni's pungent blue cheese flavor while boosting its nutritional properties.

Fresh pesto and soup are made daily; house-made bacon is cured in passion fruit syrup and rosemary; and whole, fresh pork butt is made into sausage that is served on pizza and in daily specials such as calzones, sandwiches and Stromboli.

KĪLAUEA FISH MARKET

4270 Kīlauea Rd., Kīlauea
808-828-6244
places.singleplatform.com/kilauea-fish-m
Fresh Fish and Pokē

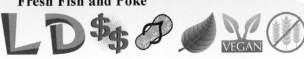

L D $$ 👡 🍃 VEGAN ⊘

Owner Corinea MacNeil trained to be a chef in France. When she moved to Kaua'i, she wanted to make fresh, healthy food with local ingredients and good flavor. In 1993, she opened the Kīlauea Fish Market located in the historic stone building of Kīlauea Sugar Plantation. After helping with the build-out, Steve Knox became a partner and the two opened the Waipouli location in 2011.

Nearly everything is made from scratch at this island-style deli that features salads, wraps and "plates." Cajun Seared 'Ahi Sashimi Salad is piled on local baby greens and comes with a side of Sesame Island Dressing as well as Shoyu Hot Mustard dipping sauce. Plates include grilled Hawaiian fish, grass-fed filet mignon, habanero chili pepper chicken, Hawaiian chili pepper pork and tofu Mexi bowl with house-made beans. Sides include brown or white rice and either a local green salad or a mac salad.

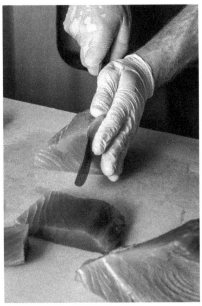

Every day they cut fresh caught fish for the market

Raw beef, fish and nine house-made sauces are available for purchase, including Sesame Island Dressing, Sesame-Soy Ginger, Shoyu Hot Mustard, Teriyaki, Creamy Garlic Cilantro, Wasabi Cream, Salsa, mild Korean-style Sesame Soy Ginger with local chili peppers and a fiery Habanero Sauce.

Grilled fresh (and usually local) habaneros are the base of the habanero sauce. They're simmered in olive oil and garlic, strained and blended. Leftover oil is reserved for customers who request that their fish, meat or tofu be cooked with it.

Their sesame 'ahi poke is a revelation. Succulent cubes of sashimi grade 'ahi are cut so there are no tough white membranes, which are a deal-breaker for me. The texture is silky, creamy and slightly firm. The 'ahi is then lightly dressed with sesame oil, Hawaiian sea salt and scallions. If you've never had poke before, make this your first.

"All poke is not created equal," says Kapa'a Store Manager Sheryl Knox, who is Steve's mother and serves about 300 pounds of fish a week. "Local fishermen deliver various kinds of whole 'ahi, so it's extremely fresh and the color ranges from deep red to pink. We make it fresh once or twice a day."

NA TERRACE

Regis Princeville Resort
20 Ka Haku Road, Princeville
08-826-2746
www.StRegisPrinceville.com/Dining/Makana-Terrace
Hawai'i Regional Cuisine

BD$$$⏰👡🍃

There's indoor seating at Makana Terrace, but Dan and I always prefer the outdoor patio that juts above the ocean. Stout Greek columns frame the Hanalei Mountains, which are mirrored in reflection pools, as waves gently crash into Hanalei Bay. There's usually a blazing sunset that gives everything a warm, orange glow.

Delicious desserts with a view of Hanalei Bay

Fish at Makana Terrace is fresh and the highlight of a carefully crafted menu, which includes fantastic sushi. Menu items have included the Makana Terrace Roll, which is sumptuous with glistening cubes of spicy tuna, crunchy tempura shrimp and creamy avocado drizzled with siracha aioli and unagi sauce. Pair an opulent sushi platter with a glass of Konteki sake and you're in heaven. Made at one of Japan's smallest breweries, the Daiginjo is the pinnacle of sake brewing.

Plump prawns are marinated in a coconut chili sauce and served on a white cheddar polenta. Mosaics of complex flavors unite in a lobster sausage, which is rolled in nori and coddled by smoldering coconut sauce.

Sake-Soy Glazed Butterfish is gorgeous in its simplicity. It's not a type of fish, but rather, a typical preparation here in Hawai'i, also known as misoyaki, which means "miso – grill" in Japanese. Any firm-fleshed fish will work in the marinade made with miso and soy sauce. When cooked, the fish has a light caramelized coating and sweet favor. At Makana Terrace, the butterfish is placed over poached baby carrots, asparagus and baby bok choy. A light kombu broth, the color of sun-filled honey, is spooned into the base.

Weekend brunch includes breakfast cocktails and house-baked pastries. Build your own Bloody Mary at the Aloha Mary bar, which includes a variety of Hawaiian sea salts. Salads have included with local heart of palm, arugula and passion fruit vinaigrette; plates of locally sourced fruit such as banana, pineapple, papaya, avocado, kiwi and citrus; and yogurt parfaits with Anahola Granola. Meals have included Costal Harbor Salmon lox, smoked ono, as well as a Hawaiian inspired omelet with tomatoes and mushrooms from the Big Island, Maui onions, Moloka'i sweet potatoes and avocados from O'ahu.

Mediterranean Gourmet

5-7132 Kūhiō Hwy., Hā'ena
808-826-9875
www.KauaiMedGourmet.com
Mediterranean with a Hawaiian Twist

Located at the Hanalei Colony Resort, Mediterranean Gourmet sits on a patch of grass overlooking the ocean. Inside, distressed red tile and colorful curtains give it a distinct Middle Eastern feel. Folds of sequined cloth billow in the breezy dining room and sometimes whales can be seen breaching in the distance.

"We take foods from around the Mediterranean—Lebanon, Greece, Spain, France and Italy—and blend them with fresh influences from Hawai'i," says Yarrow Beydoun, managing owner and wife of Imad, the chef.

Imad grew up in Beirut, Lebanon, and his favorite comfort food is Lahkme Benadora, a finely diced, grass-fed flank steak that is marinated in a seven-spice blend and cooked with tomatoes, fresh jalapeño and red onions.

"It's one of those dishes that you just dig into with your hands and a piece of pita bread," Yarrow says of the stew-like mixture that is served on a bed of ginger hummus.

"I've been eating hummus all my life, and I just thought, 'Let's try it with ginger!'" says Imad, who also makes a sun-dried tomato hummus and a curry hummus.

Menu items may include appetizers such as babaganoush and grilled kafta (spiced beef mixed with parsley and onions); wraps loaded with house-made falafel, vegetables and tahini sauce; and gyros filled with beef or lamb, vegetables and tzatziki sauce.

Phyllo dough is filled with spinach, onions, feta and sumac. "Sumac is ground berries and they are very good for you," Imad says. "There are thousands of spices in the markets back home. My mom grinds them by hand and sends them to me.

"I remember my mom putting me on a chair and I would stir everything," recalls Imad. "When I was 10, she showed me how to cut tomatoes and squeeze them with my hands for the lubia (a rice dish with green beans.) Food was fun in my house!"

Extensive wine selections offers more than 60 varieties of wine and on Wednesday evenings, take advantage of Half Price Wine Night!

NALU KAI GRILL & BAR

St. Regis Princeville Resort
5520 Ka Haku Road, Princeville
808-826-9644
www.StRegisPrinceville.com/Dining/Nalu-Kai-Grill-And-Bar
Poolside Lunch and Tapas

Nalu Kai, a casual outdoor restaurant that faces Hanalei Bay, is tucked alongside the pool of the St. Regis Resort. You wouldn't know it was there unless you went through the hotel, and even then you might miss it. At the north end of the pool, wicker chairs and glass-topped tables are lined under a gazebo; its corners draped with white curtains, tied at their center. Hawaiian music fills the small dining area. The hidden gem is open for lunch, but from May through September, and again in December, the St. Regis opens the restaurant during the evening and serves small plates. You don't have to be a guest and there's complementary valet parking.

The food at Nalu Kai looks as good as it tastes

Previous tapas have featured Nalu Kai Flatbread with a French onion spread, bacon, tender curls of Kaua'i Shrimp, mozzarella and kale salad. Prosciutto Mini Crab Cakes are served with red pepper mayonnaise, Napa cabbage remoulade and San Daniele ham crisps. Nori Panko Crusted 'Ahi Tuna includes Mediterranean slaw and citrus sriracha aioli. Chorizo Spice Crusted 'Ahi Tuna is served with a "Herbes de Provence" rice cake and sangria-glazed black mission figs. A square of Black Angus Braised Short Rib is topped with caramelized Maui onions, sautéed oyster mushrooms, a savory brown sauce and shaved Parmesan cheese.

As the sun sets over Hanalei Bay, stars pierce bright holes in the sky. Torch flames dance on the breeze as couples dine in cabanas lining the perimeter of the restaurant. White hibiscus and plumeria trees cradle them in showy privacy. You can see a picture of the Nalu Kai scene on the back cover of this book!

"It's St Regis, but it's a really fun concept," says Executive Sous Chef Maxime Michaud. "It's open to any kind of clientele, families, couples. They come here and watch the sunset, have a couple of drinks, and a couple of tapas. They're sharing everything. It's a really cool ambiance."

The sunset views from Nalu Kai can take your breath away

NAMAHANA CAFE

Kaua'i Mini Golf
5-2723 Kūhiō Hwy., Kīlauea
808-828-2118
www.NamahanaCafe.org
Hot Dogs, Burgers and Wraps

Namahana Cafe is located at Kaua'i Mini Golf, which is part of the Anaina Hou Community Park. There is a farmers market on Mondays and Saturdays and the course at Kaua'i Mini Golf winds through a 2.5-acre Hawaiian history garden. You can also walk or rent a bike and ride the Wai Koa Loop Trail, a 5-mile unpaved intermediate trail that passes by local farms and offers lush views at Stone Dam Lookout.

After enjoying the outdoor activities, you can browse the gift shop, which offers local art and Kaua'i Made products such as Kaua'i Coffee, Monkeypod Jam, Wai'ale'ale Kava, and Second Skin Naturals mosquito repellant. Cozy up on the couch and use the free Wi-Fi, or peruse an extensive book collection about Hawai'i's history, food and plants. If you prefer, order an organic, Free Trade espresso that is freshly ground to order at Namahana Cafe and sit in the outside dining area with a lush forest view.

The small cafe uses local produce from the farmers market and serves burritos, bagels, hot dogs and burgers. Bruddah Dave's Taro Burgers, made by North Shore resident Dave McEntee, are served on soft taro buns. Other locally made products include Sal's Salsa, Kaua'i Farmacy tea, Ono Pops, Kaua'i Papaya Salsa, Kaua'i Fresh Farms cucumbers, tomatoes, lettuce, kale and bananas. Eight flavors of Papalani Gelato (see page 134 for full listing) are also available.

FREE GOLF

ANAINA HOU COMMUNITY PARK IS A 15-ACRE PROPERTY THAT INCLUDES A KAUA'I BUS PARK-AND-RIDE, SKATE PARK AND HI5, 5-CENT BEVERAGE REDEMPTIONS. KAUA'I MINI GOLF IS FREE FOR HAWAI'I RESIDENTS ON THE LAST SUNDAY OF EVERY MONTH.

NANEA RESTAURANT & BAR

Westin Princeville Ocean Resort Villas
3838 Wyllie Road, Princeville
808-827-8808
www.WestinPrinceville.com/Dining/Nanea
Hawai'i Regional Cuisine

Nanea, the Westin Princeville's premier restaurant, offers poolside dining, elegantly prepared meals and heaping portions. Menu items are laced with super-foods, part of an initiative to promote wellness in all Westin Hotels & Resorts. A cornerstone of this philosophy is food synergy. When certain foods are combined, science suggests they are more beneficial than when eaten alone. Super-foods are high in nutrition and include garlic, blueberries, ginger, dark chocolate, green tea, cinnamon and onions.

Breakfast items have included Apple Banana Waffles with local bananas and dark chocolate sauce. Thick slabs of Guava Mascarpone French Toast are drizzled with cinnamon coconut syrup and scattered with blueberries.

Sunday brunch adds prime rib, sushi, Kālua Pork Benedict, Chinese Steamed Fish and Crispy Ginger Chicken to the regular offerings of eggs, bacon and sausage.

Lunch items have included the Hanalei Taro Wrap with feta cheese, garlic hummus, sprouts, avocado, lettuce, roasted peppers and tomato; 'Ahi Poke Nachos with edamame guacamole; and Short Rib Loco Moco with braised beef.

Dinner entrées have included 'Ahi Katsu, which is dipped in tempura batter, dredged in panko breadcrumbs and deep-fried. It's served with jasmine rice, sautéed bok choy, ogonori (seaweed), tomato slaw with micro greens and four sauces including kabayaki butter, green scallion oil, miso ginger and red chili oil.

Beef tenderloin is rubbed with Kaua'i Coffee and seared. It's topped with macadamia nut pesto and served with asparagus, mashed Yukon gold potatoes, Madeira jus and a balsamic reduction. The Entrée Tasting option allows you to choose two demi portions from the dinner and Fresh Sheet (fresh fish preparations) menus.

There is live entertainment every Monday and Wednesday and the Westin Princeville Jazz and Wine Festival is held every September on the resort's main lawn, which overlooks the Pacific Ocean.

The Braddah's BBQ Burger is enormously delicious at North Shore General Store

NORTH SHORE GENERAL STORE

Inside the Chevron Gas Station
5-4280 Kūhiō Hwy, Princeville
808-826-7992
www.PizzaKauai.com
American and Hawaiian

If you think eating good food at a gas station isn't an option, the North Shore General Store just may change your mind. Breakfast includes espressos made with Lavazza Super Crema whole beans and Loco Moco comes with rice, two eggs, house-made brown gravy and a grass-fed beef burger.

"All of our burgers and steak plates are made from North Shore Kaua'i Beef," says owner Darron White of the locally raised and slaughtered product that is also vacuum-sealed and available for purchase. "It's a healthier beef. There are no antibiotics, steroids, or hormones and it comes from right down the street."

Unique and tasty five-ounce burgers are served on a Passion Bakery (see page 71 for full listing) taro brioche bun and include the Sombrero with ham, cheese, a fried egg, house-made salsa verde, onion and Kaua'i Fresh Farms lettuce and tomato. The Meanest Veggie Burger piles lettuce, tomatoes and onions on a freshly made falafel patty with a drizzle of tahini sauce. House-made marinara, provolone cheese and pepperoni top the Pizza Burger, and the Chili Pepper Burger comes with house-made chili pepper sauce, house-made honey-wasabi coleslaw, lettuce, tomato and onion.

My husband, a burger connoisseur, has a new North Shore favorite. Braddah's BBQ Burger is enormously delicious and loaded with two strips of crisp bacon, two beer battered onion rings, barbecue sauce and cheese. Kimchi Teriyaki Cheeseburger is a tasty bombshell with teriyaki sauce, cheese, kimchi, sriracha and a fried egg.

Calzones and pizzas are baked in a brick oven and include house-made marinara and house-made dough. If you like thin crust, ask for hand-tossed, but if you like cracker-thin crust, ask for "thin crust." Pizza specials run every night and house pies include Pesto (with house-made pesto), The Works, Paniolo Chicken, Vinny's Teriyaki Chicken and Bacon Mushroom Onion Cheeseburger.

"When you put good quality food in someone's stomach, and you see that smile on their face, you know you're feeding people's souls," says Darron, who also sends the North Shore General Store lunch truck to Anini Beach on weekdays.

PACO'S TACOS

Kīlauea Crossings
4460 Ho'oku Road, Kīlauea
808-822-9944
Mexican

Paco's Tacos has multiple locations on the island, but their main one is located in Kapa'a. If you turn to page 68, you can read the complete description.

Baja Fish Tacos with a creamy cilantro sauce at Paco's Tacos

PERFECT PESTO

A BETTER PRODUCT, LOWER COST AND LESS LANDFILL WASTE IS WHAT PROMPTED THOMAS PICKETT OF KĪLAUEA BAKERY & PAU HANA PIZZA TO GROW BASIL FOR THE BAKERY'S MACADAMIA NUT PESTO. THOMAS FOUND A VARIETY THAT DOESN'T GO TO SEED AND OVER THE COURSE OF THREE YEARS, PLANTED 300 OF THEM. THIS SAVES THE BAKERY ABOUT $3,000 A YEAR.

PALATE WINE BAR

Located in the Historic Kong Lung Center
2474 Keneke Street, Kīlauea
808-212-1974
www.palatewinebar.net
Small Plates

Palate Wine Bar is a terrific place to relax with family and friends and enjoy esoteric wine, craft beer, or sake, and share flavorful cheese, cured meat and handmade flatbreads. If you like what you drink at Palate, you can buy it next door at Palate Market.

"We really wanted out guests to be comfortable," says General Manager Drew Thoeny of the intimate and air-conditioned space. "All of our chairs have backs and cushions. They are adjustable and we have foot stands attached to the tables. Wine and food need to be savored and this is a place where you can really enjoy it."

Chefs work in the open kitchen making flatbread to order. Dough is made every day, using a three-step rising process. Then its rolled really flat and cooked for seven minutes in 500-degree electric ovens that heat from the top and bottom. A popular choice is the Mac Nut Pesto, with fresh basil, macadamia nuts, sun-dried tomatoes and feta and mozzarella cheeses. Under it all, the crust is crunchy and thin.

Cheese and cured meat options change regularly. The Four Cheese Board has included semi-soft fluer de lait, smooth and creamy cambozola, which tastes like a triple brie and blue stilton; flakey mimolette, which is sweet and nutty; and salty but subtle Manchego. The Four Meats Board has included thin slices of mild coppa, prosciutto, chorizo sorta and chorizo blanco. If you can't decide, try the Palate Sampler Board, which comes with cheese, meat, house-made mustard, fruit, crostini and fruit compote.

"A perfect evening can be spent with us," says John Paul Gordon, chef de cuisine of both Palate Wine Bar and nearby The Bistro (see page 20 for full listing). "Shop the farmers market at 4:30 p.m. on Thursday afternoon, then have a glass of wine and appetizer at Palate, followed by dinner at The Bistro."

Sampler Board with imported cheese, cured meats, olives, housemade mustard and pickles, crostini and fruit compote

TAHITI NUI

5-5134 Kūhiō Hwy., Hanalei
(808) 826-6277
www.TheNui.com
Hawaiian and American

Tahiti Nui's humble beginnings started in 1963 when Bruce Marston and his wife, Louise Teupo'otehereri'i Hauata Marston, opened a bar and Tahitian curio shop in Hanalei. Bruce, a lieutenant colonel in the Air Force from Pasadena, California, was in Tahiti enjoying rest and recuperation when he met Louise, a native of the island.

"Louise was the person who was most responsible for keeping Tahiti Nui going," Christian Hauata Marston says of his mother who passed in 2003. "She had a way with people. It didn't matter if it was their first or second time to Tahiti Nui. She'd run around and make them a lei. It's mind-boggling to me. When I want to make a lei for somebody's birthday, it's a big deal, but she did it every day! People who came back to Kaua'i came back to Tahiti Nui especially to see her."

Today, her smiling face graces the restaurant's walls and prominent media have given Tahiti Nui a trendy boost. Part of *The Descendants*, a 2011 film set in Hawai'i starring George Clooney, was shot at Tahiti Nui. Jill Marie Landis, a Hanalei resident and author of the hilarious *Tiki Goddess Mystery Series*, opens the first book, *Mai Tai One On*, with a death in the imu pit at the Tiki Goddess Bar.

"Jill, her husband, and I are the best of friends from way back," says Marston. "Tahiti Nui definitely inspired her books and we do have an imu pit for our [Wednesday] lū'au."

Whole hogs from M&H Kaneshiro Farm in Oma'o are cooked in an imu modeled after the traditional Hawaiian underground oven. Pigs are sprinkled with sea salt, wrapped in banana and ti leaves and cooked for up to eight hours. This type of cooking, called kālua, renders succulent pork that's smoky and salty. Tahiti Nui's kālua pig is available on a sandwich with house-made barbecue sauce, as well as on Da Hui, a pizza with house-made crust, garlic butter and pineapple.

Only organic chicken, dairy and eggs are used at Tahiti Nui. Fresh and sweet Kaua'i Shrimp, which are farm-raised in Kekaha, are served with macadamia honey sauce and steamed bok choy.

The family also owns iTi Winebar, which is located next door and features more than 50 types of wine. The tapas menu (available until 11:30 p.m.) includes homemade pasta, local beef and fresh island fish.

Christian Hauata Marston

TIKI INIKI

Princeville Shopping Center
5-4280 Kūhiō Hwy., Princeville
808-431-4242
www.TikiIniki.com
Hawai'i Regional Cuisine

Rock stars Todd and Michele Rundgren opened Tiki Iniki in October 2013. The tiki bar and restaurant promises a colorful atmosphere, good food and a cocktail menu created by Julie Reiner, who was raised in Honolulu and is the force behind some of New York City's most revered cocktail bars.

"Everyone who works at Tiki Iniki knows they are hosting a party," says Michele, "and our guests should feel like they're a guest at a party in my home. Wigs are encouraged and Hawaiian attire is appreciated!"

Michele Gray first met Todd Rundgren when she was in a band called The Tubes. Todd, a vocalist and musician, produced one of their records. The Tubes are best known for their 1983 song, "She's a Beauty," which reached No. 1 on Billboard. Todd, who still tours, is best known for his songs "Hello It's Me," "I Saw The Light" and "Bang The Drum All Day."

Thanks to Michele's background in show business, Tiki Iniki looks like a movie set with tiki wood sculptures (two from 1940s Trader Vic's in Honolulu) and hand-carved tiki bar stools. Colorful buoy-inspired lights hang from a ceiling covered in flame-retardant coconut fronds. A lava wall resembles what Michele saw on the Big Island and chairs from the original Don the Beachcomber have been reupholstered.

Tiki collectibles from the Rundgrens—as well as those donated by friends—fill every nook and cranny. Artifacts from Coco Palms include fake coconuts from the *Pirates of the Caribbean* set, a giant wood sculpture and a tear-shaped orange chandelier. An arched hut is shaped like the legendary resort's entrance and the deck is the same shape as the Coco Palms' lobby. In the dining room, chefs work behind a shiny, stainless steel open kitchen with a Wood Stone oven.

"We offer fine dining, comfort food, pūpū and a late-night menu with noodles and pizza," says Michele. "I'm a huge football fan so we'll open earlier during the season, and Spam hamburgers will definitely be on the menu!"

Classic and modern style tiki drinks are in abundance at Tiki Iniki

TRUCKING DELICIOUS

Next to Hanalei Liquor Store
5-5100 Kūhiō Hwy., Hanalei
808-482-4101

Hawaiian

Chloe Sorey opened Trucking Delicious in March 2014, nearly two years after graduating from the Culinary Arts Program at Kaua'i Community College (KCC). She was born and raised in Hanalei, attended Hanalei and Kapa'a schools and catered her first wedding at the age of 15. From ages 16 to 19, she attended KCC while working at Bar Acuda Restaurant in Hanalei. After graduation, she moved to O'ahu and took more cooking classes at Kapi'olani Community College.

"When Chloe was two, my grandmother and I set her on the kitchen floor with a vinyl tablecloth and gave her a bowl of noodles and sauce," recalls mother Julie Sorey, who helps Chloe with her business. "She ate it and got it all over the walls and herself. When she was four, we started making Greek food together."

Those early experiences sculpted Chloe's penchant for pairing unexpected ingredients that blend sweet, salty, bitter, sour and umami (savory). After specializing in gourmet grilled cheese sandwiches, Chloe changed her menu in Jan. 2016. Today, she takes "local food" up a notch and makes gourmet plate lunch.

Chloe likes to be challenged, so menu items change frequently. The current lunch menu includes Kaua'i Shrimp sautéed in a secret sauce that contains garlic, lime juice and chili peppers and a scrumptious bacon and egg fried rice served with three wontons and house smoked meat with salted onions.

"Learning how to smoke meat the traditional way has

Chloe Sorey

been a process," says Chloe of the eight-hour process. "Local guys always ask me who smokes my meat because no one expects that I do it."

Wonton of the Week includes seven fat wontons stuffed with things like seared and smoked 'ahi in cream cheese and Okinawan sweet potatoes with bacon, green onions, pepper jack cheese and candied jalapeños.

A variety of desserts are also made fresh every day and have included ube (purple sweet potato) ice cream with chunks of young coconut sandwiched between white chocolate macadamia nut cookies and liliko'i (passion fruit) cheesecake with fresh strawberries.

Saimin Saturday features house-made char su in a broth-y noodle soup.

Warung Bali

Hanalei farmers market
808-779-3809
www.WBaliFood.com
Balinese Food

I had my slippahs blown off when I interviewed Yantini Wood of Warung Bali. It was a lazy, sun-filled afternoon and we were at her home in Kīlauea. I had nothing to go on except an invitation from Matt Wood to try his wife's fare. After one bite, I was seduced by the fresh, light Balinese cuisine layered with intense flavor.

Historically, Chinese and Europeans called Indonesia the "Spice Islands" for its vibrant nutmeg, mace and clove trade. Indonesian cuisine is diverse, in part because the country is composed of some 6,000 populated islands. The dishes of Eastern Indonesia are similar to those in Polynesia and Melanesia, often featuring sweet potatoes, taro, cassava and breadfruit.

"When you live in Bali, all the women have to know how to cook," explains Yantini, who was born and raised in eastern Bali, a province of Indonesia. Her accent was thick but her soft voice was light, joyful and patient as she struggled to find the right words. "When I was 10 years old, I began helping my mother cook food that she sold at the farmers market."

Yantini uses family recipes along with farmers market produce and local fish to expertly weave spice into her food. On her table, fragrant aromas rose from a large platter. Banana leaves were folded into little bowls and loaded with enticing meat, fish, noodles and vegetables. Four condiments allowed me to add as little or as much heat as I wanted.

Her recipes are vast, but include pork satay made with pork shoulder, freshly ground coriander, white pepper, lemongrass and kaffir lime leaves. Chicken larb is made with toasted rice, kaffir lime leaf, soy sauce, sesame oil, tomatoes, shallots and lemongrass.

My favorite dish is Chicken with Balinese Sauce. Chicken breasts are poached in turmeric, garlic, lemongrass and salam leaf, also known as Indonesian laurel. After it's cooled, Yantini shreds the chicken and mixes it with fresh lemongrass, garlic, ginger and shallots. The dish is outstanding and located at the top of my Last Meal list.

Shrimp Pad Thai with peanut, tamarind and garlic from Warung Bali

EAST SIDE

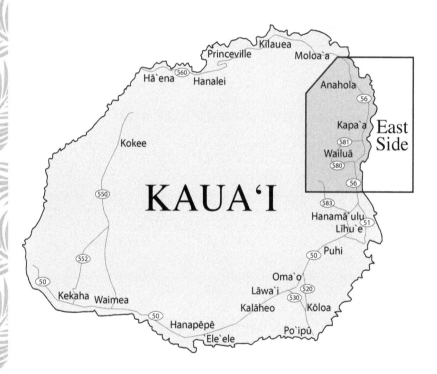

Palm trees on the East Side give the area the name of the Royal Coconut Coast

AL PASTOR

Kūhiō Highway, across from Products Fair, Kapa'a
808-652-6953
www.Facebook.com/AlPastorTacos.Kauai
Mexican

In Spain, "al pastor" means "shepherd style," a cooking technique known as huli huli (to turn over) in Hawai'i. Meat is cooked over a spit that rotates over a heat source, and as the fat drips, it bastes the meat. At Al Pastor, Paulino Hernandez soaks pork in a guajillo chili marinade overnight. In the morning, he stacks it onto the spit of an al pastor machine and roasts it until it drips with juice and crackles with flavor.

The signature dish is two Al Pastor Tacos with a side of soupy pinto beans and Spanish rice. The meat is saturated in a fatty juice that blends with the marinade and drips down your hand if you let it.

Everything is made fresh every day, including the beans. If you like your food fiery, ask for a side of hot sauce. Paulino makes a different one every day, and blends have included deep-red chipotle, green habanero and spicy serrano.

Fish tacos include two generous portions of lightly grilled fish, folded into soft corn tortillas and topped with crisp lettuce and a smoky chipotle cream sauce.

Paulino's cheerful wife Faun delivers orders with a smile, and if she has time, will happily sit down and talk story.

Faun always takes orders with a smile at Al Pastor

ART CAFÉ HEMINGWAY

4-1495 Kūhiō Hwy., Kapaʻa
808-822-2250
www.ArtCafeHemingway.com
Light European

BLD $$ 👙 🍃 🌾 📶

Markus and Jana Boemer once owned Leica Gallery Prague, in the Prague Castle Supreme Burgrave, which included a small café. The gallery became very popular and politically relevant in the Czech Republic. A new presidency forced the gallery's closure, but they came up with a clever idea to bring art to the people. Photo exhibits by artists such as Salgado, Antonín Kratochvíl and Wim and Donata Wenders toured Eastern Europe on three Czech Railway carriages.

In 2010, the Boemers sold their portable gallery, moved to Kauaʻi, and opened a large café with a small gallery. Jana (pronounced Yana) has always been an inspired cook, and the menu reflects her taste in high-quality ingredients. The couple buys the best coffee, tea and ingredients they can find, and makes almost everything from scratch—including mayonnaise. They also source as much local and organic produce as possible, shop the Kapaʻa farmers market every Wednesday and grow herbs in a small garden.

Recently, the couple partnered with Jeremiah Merriman. "Hemingway by Miah" is open Mon. through Wed. and "Hemingway by Markus and Jana" is open Thurs. through Sun.

It doesn't matter which day you go, the food is always terrific. The small, European-inspired menu is filled with crepes, deli meats such as pancetta, and scrambled eggs made with Parmigiano-Reggiano cheese. The Sun Also Rises includes fresh orange juice, scrambled eggs with Parmegiano Reggiano, smoked ham, Camembert, baguette slices as well as whole grain bread and butter. Baguettes are made fresh daily and you can take a hot one home if you order at least 30 minutes in advance.

Lunch includes baked chicken flavored with cinnamon, ginger and tomatoes. Dinner includes fondue, the house special, made with Swiss cheeses and white wine. Another option is seared Kauaʻi prawns with kaffir lime curry and rice. A small cocktail menu includes wine, prosecco, mimosas and Bloody Marys. Fresh coconut water, fresh squeezed orange juice and great cups of espresso are fantastic options for those who do not drink.

The bright, charming atmosphere is roomy and neat and parking is across the street.

Markus just may make the best espresso on the island

Mason jar mango cobbler at Caffé Coco

CAFFÉ COCO

4-369 Kūhiō Hwy., Wailuā
808-822-7990
www.CaffeCocoKauai.com
Fresh and Healthy

Hollan and Haleem Hamid bought Caffé Coco from former owner Ginger Carlson in 2011. Now, it features tableside service, new chairs, white tablecloths and votive candles. At night, tiki torches and twinkle lights add a tropical backyard feel.

"Caffé Coco has been around for so long (since 2006), I wanted to keep the good parts," explains Hollan, "and change the menu so we could support local farmers. If I can't get ingredients from Kaua'i, then I get it from the state. To me, that's important. It tastes better, and it's better for the planet."

Hollan is a strict vegan who's restricted to a gluten-free diet, and the tasty menu reflects that. Fresh, organic and local ingredients are transformed into colorful, nutrient-dense meals that satisfy and nourish. If the words "gluten-free" and "vegan" put you off, don't worry. You don't have to be on an alternative diet to enjoy the food. There is also fresh fish, organic chicken and shrimp.

A keiki (children's) menu includes fish and rice, cheese quesadillas, pasta with butter and Parmesan, and grilled cheese sandwiches. "It's food kids like," says Hollan, who also caters weddings and teaches vegan workshops, "but we serve it with organic carrots and cucumbers so it's a little healthy."

During breakfast and lunch, Hollan opens Hippie Cafe, which is inside Caffé Coco. Items include açaí bowls, smoothies, baked goods and salads. Cold-brewed coffee, fresh coconut water and tea round out the beverage options.

The outside dining area is festive and features live music most nights. A nontoxic citronella and peppermint formula is sprayed to keep the bugs at a minimum, but bugs come with outside dining, so wear bug juice or long pants.

KAPA'A TRAFFIC

YOU MAY WANT TO CONSIDER THE TRAFFIC IN KAPA'A WHILE YOU'RE PLANNING YOUR DAY. IT CAN GET PRETTY BACKED UP FROM WAILUĀ THROUGH OLD KAPA'A TOWN. WHAT NORMALLY TAKES 5 MINUTES, COULD TAKE UP TO ONE HOUR. RUSH HOUR USUALLY OCCURS BETWEEN 11 A.M. AND 1 P.M. AND AGAIN BETWEEN 4 AND 6 P.M.

COCONUT CUP JUICE BAR & CAFE

4-1516 Kūhiō Hwy., Kapa'a
808-823-8630
www.CoconutCupJuiceBar.com
Fresh and Healthy

BLD $ 🩴 🍃 🌱 VEGAN 🌾

If you're in the mood for light, healthy food, Coconut Cup is an excellent choice. Owner Christa Hall uses organic ingredients whenever possible and maintains a network of local farmers to keep her menu fresh and flavorful. Order at the takeout window and eat outside at green picnic tables shaded by red umbrellas.

Sandwiches, wraps and salads are loaded with vegetables and the gourmet sandwiches are a handful. Close to 4 inches thick and made with fresh-baked whole wheat bread, you just might have leftovers. Sandwiches include Black Forest ham or turkey breast, albacore tuna and avocado veggie.

Fresh-baked muffins and big fat cookies from Passion Bakery (see page 71 for full listing) line the outside bar. Handmade signs advertise homemade pesto hummus with organic corn chips or red pepper hummus on a bagel with fresh veggies.

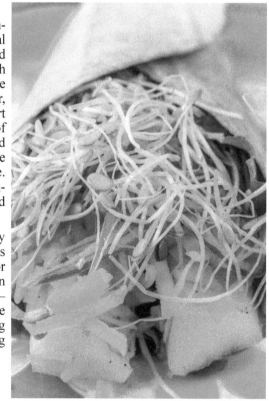

You can get a shot of fresh-pressed wheatgrass or local organic honey with kava and cacao. Smoothies are made with local fruit, and extras include spirulina, ionized alkaline water, rice milk, soymilk, açaí, yogurt and protein powder. Glasses of fresh-squeezed juice are based on what's in season, and the Kombucha tea is made in house. Shave ice is made with fresh-squeezed fruit juice and no added sugar.

Not only is the food healthy at Coconut Cup, but also Hall's business practices are healthy for the island. She is listed as a green business with Mālama Kaua'i—pledging to be a steward of the island by reducing waste, using green supplies and supporting local farms.

Fresh hummus and cucumber wrap

GOPAL'S CRÊPERIE

4-1620 Kūhiō Hwy., Kapa'a
808-635-2164
www.facebook.com/GopalsCreperie
Gluten-free Crepes, Ice Cream and Tea

Located across the street from the Kaua'i Products Fair in Kapa'a, steady streams of customers come to this tiny lunch wagon for sweet and savory gluten-free crepes. Each 12-inch crepe is generously loaded with fresh and flavorful fillings, some of which are made with farmers market produce. All fillings are made from scratch and all crepes are gluten-free, vegetarian and absolutely delicious.

"I'm an artist at heart," owner Indy Reeves says. She's a Hare Krishna who named her place after Gopal, the sustainer of cows and cattle and the infant and child form of Lord Krishna. "Every crepe I make is a little piece of art. I blend it with my spirituality by offering the crepe to Krishna that's in every customer's heart."

We spoke while sitting at a small, round table in the crêperie's outside dining area. Next to us, a young couple ate a late afternoon lunch under a gazebo with a view of the ocean, nearly 50 yards away. A triple strand of mala beads hung low on Indy's neck and the ocean breeze blew tight curls from her long ponytail.

Indy spent six months perfecting her recipe for gluten-free batter, and it's really good. There are no eggs or gluten to give the crepes their classic, springy and delicate texture, but they are crisp, tender and tasty. Plus, there's none of the cloying aftertaste that often coats your tongue after eating most gluten-free products.

Our favorite savory crepes include hearty gingered lentil with feta cheese, sun-dried tomato pesto with feta cheese; and basil pesto with feta cheese. If we want something a little sweeter, we go for the fresh-made macadamia nut butter, slices of apple bananas and a drizzle of local honey, or stewed pineapples with honey, goat cheese and ginger.

"WE DEVELOP MENUS BY PAIRING SEASONAL INGREDIENTS AT THEIR PEAK PERFECTION, WHICH IS IN ESSENCE, EXPLORING WHAT HAWAI'I REGIONAL CUISINE REALLY IS. I LOVE USING HANAPĒPĒ SEA SALT BECAUSE IT MAKES ME APPRECIATE THE SIMPLICITY IN GREAT COOKING. KAUA'I HAS THE HIGHEST QUALITY INGREDIENTS AND POTENTIAL TO BE A MECCA FOR CHEFS AND DINERS ALIKE."

COLLIN DARRELL, CO-OWNER, HANAI MARKET

HAOLE GIRL ISLAND SWEETS

Kinipopo Shopping Center
4-356 Kūhiō Hwy.
808-822-2253
www.haolegirlsweets.com
Fresh and Healthy

"The name is a spoof because I'm a wanna be native," says Judy Palmer, who has pale skin, bright blue eyes and curly red hair.

Eighteen years ago, Judy—a graduate of the Culinary Institute of America (CIA) in Hyde Park, NY—helped reopen Princeville Resort after Hurricane Iniki damaged it. She was the featured pastry chef at the 2004 James Beard Awards and in 2000; she was the executive pastry chef for the Cannes Film Festival. Today, she bakes macadamia nut sticky buns, croissants and wedding cakes with rolled fondant.

"My croissants are made with lots of butter and hand-rolled," says Palmer, whose tiny frame is surprising for someone who makes food with boatloads of butter. "I roll 64-pounds of dough twice a week, and I love it because I don't need to go to a gym!"

Other ingredients include flour, yeast, Kauaʻi honey and Hawaiian sea salt. She layers butter between the dough, folds it in three like a letter, then lets it rest for 20 minutes. The process is repeated twice and the dough is left to set overnight. In the end, each croissant has about 150 layers.

"Since there's only butter in this dough, it melts in your mouth" explains Palmer. "Some people use shortening, which has a higher melting point than your body temperature, and that's why it's gummy and tastes like a Crisco slick."

Judy Palmer

Judy twists the dough into plain butter croissants and fills some with combinations of produce that she's bought at the farmers market. Popular flavors include roasted pineapple with basil; purple sweet potato and coconut milk; caramel apple banana with macadamia nuts; chocolate apple banana; ham and cheese with Aunty Lilikoʻi Passion Fruit Mustard; Hawaiian dark chocolate and flaked coconut; portable mushroom with Havarti cheese; and sun-dried tomato and spinach with Kauaʻi Kunana Dairy goat cheese.

Besides the shop, Haole Girl Island Sweets is at the Kauaʻi Culinary Market at The Shops at Kukuiʻula (Wednesdays 3:30 to 6 p.m.), Kauaʻi Community Market (Saturdays 9:30 a.m. to 1 p.m.) and Hanapēpē Art Night Market (Fridays 6 to 9 p.m.)

HUKILAU LANAI

520 Aleka Loop, Kapa'a
808-822-0600
www.HukilauKauai.com
Hawai'i Regional Cuisine

Hukilau Lanai is one of our favorite restaurants and we always bring visiting family and friends here for their last dinner. It's located about 10 minutes from the airport and a fantastic way to end a trip if you're on an overnight flight. The Island Orchid cocktail packs a deadly punch and is responsible for making one friend miss her flight! She had fallen in love with Kaua'i and didn't want to leave, but she and her husband caught a flight the next morning.

Owners Ron and Krissi Miller maintain a consistent menu and offer nightly specials based on seasonal ingredients. A small onsite garden provides the kitchen with pungent herbs and the fish is always fresh and sourced from Hawai'i. Guests can now choose a local mixed green or arugula salad to accompany their meal without paying an upgrade charge.

Chef and owner, Ron Miller holding the day's fresh catch of yellow fin tuna

An interactive online menu lets you see what farm the food comes from, and everything is made in-house including bread, pasta and charcuterie. Adam's Poke Nachos are so delicious; *Bon Appétit* magazine requested the recipe. Our favorites include the Swiss Chard and Mushroom Tart with a homemade pie crust; mixed grill with fresh fish and sugarcane-skewered shrimp; and meatloaf made with local beef and mushrooms, served with mashed potatoes and a brown butter sauce.

A delicious five-course early-bird tasting menu is an affordable $32, or $50 with the wine paring. Pool bar lunch specials are one of the deals on Kaua'i; look for .e popular Prime Rib Au Jus Sub on fresh-made bread.

Once a week, the kitchen receives a whole hog from M & H Kaneshiro Farm in Lāwa'i. Hukilau Lanai's revolving charcuterie plate has included headcheese, summer sausage, paté and mortadella. It's not for everyone, but there's a waiting list for adventurous eaters.

Annual events such as Earth Day in April and Oktoberfest in October give the staff a chance to get hyperlocal and regional specific. Previous Oktoberfest menus have included opah schnitzel, 'ahi sauerbraten, knackwurst and bratwurst.

Honey vanilla gelato and coconut fritters

Kaua'i Shrimp and Kaneshiro pork belly croquette

JAVA KAI

4-1384 Kūhiō Hwy., Kapa'a
808-823-6887
www.JavaKaiHawaii.com
Coffee House

Java Kai is located in Old Town Kapa'a. The vibe is young, boisterous and fun, and the produce is largely organic and locally grown. Beans are roasted onsite and a giant chalkboard lists 50 coffee drinks, smoothies and Italian sodas, as well as the "word of the day." Baristas grind beans that are roasted locally and delivered weekly.

Xochitl Garcia's mother originally bought Mermaids Café and Java Kai in 1989. The coffee shop was too much, so she sold it to her daughter. Since taking over in 2009, Xochitl (her name is Aztec and is pronounced "so-chi") and her husband, Sean, have increased the staff and created a menu that goes beyond coffee.

Every morning at 4 a.m., a baker heats the ovens and makes mountains of homey pastries. If you get there when they open, rich and tender muffins and scones are warm from the oven, and the smell of cooked sugar and melted butter fills the air.

Besides coffee, espresso, tea and fresh juice, the coffee shop offers breakfast sandwiches and bagels, as well as salads and hot sandwiches for lunch or dinner.

Local artists hang their art, with new exhibits premiering at the Kapa'a Art Walk on the first Saturday of each month. Locally made jewelry and body lotions are also for sale.

This coffee shop is small and busy, but there is usually a table available inside or out front. Additional parking is available in the back, but if you're in a rush, call ahead and place your order.

The drinks at Java Kai are tasty and artistic

Jo2

4-971 Kūhiō Highway, Kapa'a
808-212-1627
www.jotwo.com
Hawai'i Regional Cuisine

Even though Jean Marie Josselin is a legendary chef who helped pioneer Hawai'i's food identity, you wouldn't know it if you watched him cook. He works quietly, tucked behind a small granite topped bar, which is open to the cozy, art-deco dining room that seats 60. A new bar and outside patio allow for more than 30 additional seats.

Jo2's small menu is built upon fresh ingredients that are transformed into whimsical vegetable-based dishes. But even though his food is playful, there's a deeper calling.

"America's food chain is not safe enough for people to trust," says Josselin explaining why he works with local farmers to source heirloom produce. "Everyone is tired of getting sick from their food. In Japan or France, they take their food chain very, very seriously and they trust it tremendously."

It's hard to categorize Jo2. It's certainly fine dining, but it's also laid-back and accessible. If Jo2 were a dish, it'd have to be Jean Marie's Domoyojiko Rice Congee. A rich crab broth is combined with creamy rice, vegetables, lemon confit, tempura crab legs and whispers of fresh ginger, making it complex, comforting and surprising.

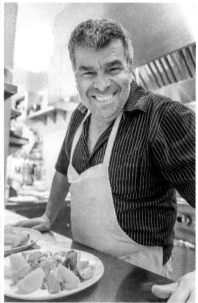

Chef Jean Marie Josselin

The menu changes often but another dish I've enjoyed is Artichoke Minestrone with tender artichoke hearts in a light tomato broth. An artful swipe of silky garlic purée and a tangle of lū'au (taro leaves) infused gnocchi, rounds of summer squash, peeled grape tomatoes and green beans are sprinkled with zesty pistou.

Binchotan Grilled Leeks are a study in rich, cool and creamy. Organic leeks are grilled over Binchotan charcoal, which doesn't smoke. What does get smoked is the cool pool of buttermilk. A nob of creamy goat cheese and XO bacon make the dish irresistible.

Seared "Hunan" style rack of lamb is immensely satisfying. Mint oil is drizzled over Colorado lamb, which is tender, juicy and robust. Not a hint of gamey flavor mucks up the meat that sits on a bed of tender carrots, fingerling potatoes, baby bok choy, artichoke hearts and a savory chipotle truffle sauce.

"I'm always trying to be ahead of the curve without being too weird," says Josselin. "It's not Pacific Rim Cuisine. It's not Hawai'i Regional Cuisine. It's my cuisine."

Oysters with passion fruit cacao shave ice

57

KALALEA JUICE HALE

4390 Pu'u Hale Loop, Anahola
808-346-0074
www.facebook.com/Kalaleajuice
Juice, Smoothies and Açaí Bowls

Near mile marker 14 in Anahola, an orange building with a hand-made sign portrays a blossoming Hawaiian woman. She's holding a glass of green juice in one hand and a basket of fruit in the other. The words "Kalalea Juice Hale" cover a painting of Kalalea Mountain and a small sign reads, "Local, Fresh, Organic."

"We are turning the table on health in my hometown of Anahola," says owner Carla Contrades-Barrett, whose Hawaiian family spans three generations. For 30 years, Carla's family ran a popular huli huli chicken stand and her mother, Kuini Contrades, made and sold lei during the spring and summer. Now she continues the tradition. Carla's husband, Lopaka Barrett, remodeled the buildings extending the family's food legacy.

Robyn Curley and Chatson Barrett

Carla opened the shop in September as an endowment for her sons, Chatson and Kawai. Chatson is a private chef and his girlfriend, Robyn Curley, is the taste tester.

Every morning at 5:30 a.m., Chatson cracks the husk off young and old coconuts. Water from young green ones will be used in the O.G. açaí bowl. Wrinkled brown ones have the most meat, which Chatson grates and presses into coconut milk and adds to Kalalea Love, a smoothie made with strawberries, bananas, peanut butter, cacao nibs and cacao powder.

The Next Level açaí bowl contains protein powder, kale, fresh coconut milk, apple bananas, chunks of fresh coconut meat, honey, bee pollen, peanut butter and granola made by Kauai Kunana Dairy.

Cold-pressed juices include Olena, with carrots, orange, turmeric and mint; Kale Cure with cucumber, kale, apple, green papaya and lemon; and Beauty in da Beets with beets, apple, ginger and basil.

Organic shave ice includes syrups made with whole fruit, and come with your choice of two flavors: lilikoʻi , strawberry, blueberry, mango, lychee, tangerine, lime, dragon fruit, banana and fruit punch.

"Buying local and organic ingredients are important to us," says Robyn. "We support the local economy by buying local. Plus, we surf, and all the pesticide runoff ends up in the ocean. We also care about the land and the health of the people."

KAUA'I JUICE CO.

4504 Kukui St., Suite 20-A, Kapa'a
808-634-0886
www.KauaiJuiceCo.com
Cold-Pressed Juice Bar

Before meeting Kristal Muhich, owner of Kaua'i Juice Co., I thought drinking kombucha (pronounced "kom boo cha") was like drinking apple cider vinegar. I didn't understand why the fermented beverage had been consumed for more than 2,000 years. But a just-opened bottle of KJC's kombucha smells fresh and sweet. The sour tang is barely noticeable and it's loaded with fizzy bubbles (a natural byproduct of fermentation) and robust fruit flavor.

"It doesn't taste sour because it's super fresh," says Kristal. "Everything is just recently bottled, unlike like most 'booch' that has been pasteurized and distributed. Probiotics are most alive within the first few weeks of inoculation. That means it's not only the tastiest, but also the most nutrient-dense. Plus, I use up to 20 percent fresh juice per bottle, which makes it way more expensive but worth it."

Kaua'i Juice Co.'s "booch" is available in stores island-wide. In the summer of 2014, Kristal and her husband, Dylan Scott, opened their first store in Kapa'a and began making cold-pressed juice. Kristal is an artist when it comes to flavor combinations and each blend bursts with mouth-watering vibrancy. I know it sound crazy to call juice "juicy," but that is the first word that comes to mind.

Kristal Muhich and Dylan Scott

"Omega This" is sunshine in a bottle and includes chia seeds, pineapple, tangerines, grapefruit, soursop, liliko'i (passion fruit) and fractionated coconut oil—which balances metabolism and increases energy. "Mo Beta" is a sweet and earthy blend of beets—which boost blood flow, muscle contraction and neurotransmission—and carrots, apple, lemon and ginger. "Mintacolada" is a sweet and refreshing blend of local pineapple, passion fruit, coconut water and mint.

Creamy and rich "Island Milk" is made with macadamia nuts, cashews, alkaline water, vanilla, agave and Hawaiian sea salt. "Best Breakfast" adds cacao and cold-brewed coffee to the Island Milk blend.

Shots include the "Everything," with moringa, a medicinal plant that's used to relieve joint pain, lower blood pressure and promote sleep. "Life Saver," made with turmeric, ginger, garlic, apple cider vinegar and Hawaiian chili peppers, promises to be the ultimate cold buster.

KAUA'I PASTA

4-939B Kūhiō Hwy., Kapa'a
808-822-7447
www.KauaiPasta.com
Italian

Kaua'i Pasta in Kapa'a serves Italian-style meals in child-friendly dining rooms. The restaurant in Līhu'e is smaller and less suited for families, but is ideal for a nice meal, or a business lunch or dinner. At both restaurants, sauces and pizza dough are made in-house and local products such as Kaua'i beef and produce are used.

The Kapa'a restaurant has two large dining rooms with Italian-themed ambiance; the swanky KP Lounge is in back. You can sit wherever you want and order from any menu. The main menu features homemade sauces such as marinara, Alfredo, macadamia nut pesto and a meat sauce made with Kaua'i beef.

Nightly specials have included Kaua'i Shrimp poached in bacon fat with local Meyer lemon béarnaise sauce and oyster mushroom ravioli, paired with Nicole Chanrion Côte-de-Brouilly.

R&B pumps through the speakers of the KP Lounge while customers sip craft beer, wine or specialty cocktails. Colorful earth tones add strokes of amber, orange and red to dark chocolate walls, and a brown leather couch is tucked behind the granite-topped bar. Sports play on the big screen with the volume turned down.

My favorite item on the KP Lounge menu is the Truffled Prawn Ramen with angel hair pasta in a spicy broth. The Truffle Parmesan Fries have a crispy, bubbled skin with creamy insides and are served with four homemade dipping sauces: Italian tomato coulis, roasted red pepper rémoulade, creamy Alfredo and cool ranch.

FRESH FISH

FRESH MEANS FOODS THAT HAVE NOT BEEN FROZEN OR PRESERVED IN ANY WAY. PEOPLE IN HAWAI'I HAVE ACCESS TO SOME OF THE FRESHEST, SAFEST AND MOST FLAVORFUL FISH ON THE PLANET. MANY RESTAURANTS BUY FROM THE HONOLULU FISH AUCTION, WHICH ONLY SELLS SUSTAINABLE HOOK-AND-LINE CAUGHT FISH THAT HAS MET THE REQUIREMENTS OF THE FOOD AND AGRICULTURE ORGANIZATION OF THE UNITED NATIONS. THERE ARE A HANDFUL OF FISHERMAN ON KAUA'I WHO SELL TO LOCAL RESTAURANTS, AND THE MENU WILL NOTE IF THEY SOURCE FROM KAUA'I'S WATERS. IF YOU DON'T SEE THE WORD "FRESH" ON THE MENU, IT'S LIKELY BECAUSE THE FISH WAS FROZEN AND IMPORTED.

KĪLAUEA FISH MARKET

4400 Aleka Place #5, Kapaʻa
808-822-3474
places.singleplatform.com/kilauea-fish-market
Fresh Fish and Pokē

The Kīlauea Fish Market has two locations on the island, but their main one is located in Kīlauea. If you turn to page 29, you can read the complete description.

Cajun Seared Ahi Sashimi Salad includes 8 ounces of blackened ahi

"MY FAVORITE LOCAL INGREDIENT IS MANGO. I LOVE TO USE IT IN BOTH SWEET AND SAVORY DISHES. I ESPECIALLY LIKE WHEN IT'S EARLY IN THE SEASON, SO I CAN MAKE TRADITIONAL PICKLED GREEN MANGO. I LIKE TO MAKE COMFORT FOODS WITH A TWIST BY PUTTING MY SPIN ON TRADITIONAL FOODS AND I LOVE ENCOURAGING PEOPLE TO TRY SOMETHING THAT'S A LITTLE OUT OF THEIR COMFORT ZONE."

CHLOE SOREY, CHEF AND OWNER, TRUCKING DELICIOUS

NTRY KITCHEN

4-1485 Kūhiō Hwy., Kapaʻa
808-822-3511
places.singleplatform.com/kountry-style-kitchen-restaurant
American and Hawaiian

BL $$ 🩴 🌿

Kountry Kitchen's exterior is painted blue and orange, with benches under an awning providing shade for the outside waiting area. Inside, is a clean, cozy diner that serves good food. Comical chicken paintings by local artist Fanny Bilodeau hang on the walls and knickknacks are tucked into every free space. Wood benches provide ample room for two, or intimate seating for four. Large windows spread across the front, giving diners a view of the highway and the ocean across the street.

The restaurant, which is only open for breakfast and brunch, is known for large portions of Island-style breakfasts and American classics. Our favorite is the Loco Moco with kālua pork instead of the traditional hamburger patty. It's a massive dish of steamed rice, brown gravy and shreds of smoky pork that have been crisped on the griddle, two fried eggs and toast. It's so large, Daniel and I usually share it.

Breakfast includes a BLT Sandwich or an Egg Sandwich (with 9 meat options, 4 cheese options and 8 vegetable options), served on an English muffin. Both come with your choice of rice or hash browns. If you're hungry for a typical American breakfast of bacon, pancakes, hash browns and eggs, you'll find it here. You can also order Grilled Mahimahi with eggs, hash browns or rice and toast; and 3 varieties of Eggs Benedict. Visitors hold the coconut syrup in high esteem and local favorites include fried rice with Portuguese sausage.

Toes-in-the-sand dining at Lava Lava Beach Club

Lava Lava Beach Club

420 Papaloa Rd., Kapaʻa
(808) 241-5282
www.LavaLavaBeachClub.com
American and Hawaiian

Lava Lava Beach Club is a 250-seat open-air restaurant and bar with tables, couches and fire-pits on the sand. Ironwood trees line the waterfront and Sleeping Giant (Nounou mountain) hugs the southern end of Wailuā Bay. Guests sit in plastic chairs along the shore, a whale breaches 200 yards away and a surfer catches some waves. Near my table, a dog on a leash sips water from a huge ceramic water bowl.

Due to the east-facing coastline, sunrise breakfasts are special. Full breakfast offerings are available until 10 a.m. and include options such as Hapa Laka Loco Moco with Portuguese sausage, local beef patty, two eggs, fried rice and mushroom gravy. The Wailuā Bay Benedict features slow roasted kālua pork, poached eggs, yuzu hollandaise and fantastic home fries.

Dinner standouts include Hook, Line & Sinker, which is based on the chef's whim, so it changes every day. Today, mahi mahi is served over mashed potatoes and edamame puree and drizzled with butter sauce; a brilliant combination. Thick slices of caramelized Hamakua mushrooms are tucked against plump shrimp and sautéed kale. A tangle of crispy leeks sits on the fish.

LLBC Burger is a sizeable patty served a perfect medium-rare with rich grass-fed flavor. It's stuffed with blue cheese and topped with avocado, fried sweet onions, tomato, arugula, cheddar cheese and chive aioli and served with sweet potato waffle fries.

You can always find fresh island fish on the menu at Lava Lava Beach Club

The bar serves a variety of beer, but if you really want to party, the Bamboocha Mai Tai is probably the only drink you'll need! Bamboocha is pidgin for "huge" and the cocktail is served in a 10-inch bamboo "glass" that you get to keep. There are more than nine variations of the Bloody Mary, including the BLT with a maple-bacon rim and a strip of bacon tucked inside.

As we wind up dinner, live Hawaiian music fills the air. The silhouette of the mountains presses against clouds that change color in the late day sun, which glints off palm trees. An airplane flies toward the airport and a cruise ship shimmies in the hazy distance. I'm disarmed by it all. It's like an enchanting movie set. This is what people expect when they come to Hawaiʻi.

MONICO'S TAQUERIA

4-356 Kūhiō Hwy., Kapaʻa
808-822-4300
www.MonicosTaqueria.com
Mexican

It's always a pleasure to be served a plate of Mexican food at Monico's where the fare is elegant and rustic--known as rustic-chic in foodie circles. Sometimes, Mexican food isn't that pretty to look at, but at Monico's, many entrées are elegantly presented and garnished with thin slivers of colorful, fresh peppers.

Owner Monico Hernandez-Martinez and his team cook in an open kitchen and kindly look over the steamy stovetop from time to time, making sure diners are happy and fed. Kathleen, Monico's wife, takes care of the business details and helps serve when the restaurant is busy.

The family-owned restaurant offers an extensive menu including taquitos, fajitas and tostadas. Burritos include the Fish Burrito with fresh fish-of-the-day, rice and beans smothered in house-made jalapeño crema as well as tender pork carnitas with house-made green sauce; sautéed fresh vegetables with house-made red sauce and guacamole; and shredded chicken with rice, beans and your choice of sauce.

Tacos include sautéed fresh catch, shredded chicken, carne asada, carnitas or al pastor served with salsa fresca, beans and rice. You'll also find burgers, quesadillas and shrimp, fish or chicken salads. The bar serves top-shelf tequila and cranks out margaritas, including a delicious passion fruit blend.

Lunch and dinner are extremely busy, so aim for off hours if you're in a hurry.

The Woody burger delivers a whole lot of flavor with a nice spicey finish at NOM

Nom Breakfast & Burgers

4-1620 Kūhiō Hwy, Kapaʻa
808-320-3349
www.nomkauai.com
Breakfast and Burgers

BLD$$ 🩴 🍃 VEGAN ⊘ 🚚

Thomas Fuquay was a chef at The Bistro in Kīlauea who wanted to do his own thing. So he quit, bought a food truck with a commercial kitchen and a friend inspired the name.

"My friend said 'You should call your food truck Tom's Bombs Noms,'" says Thomas. "I thought that was funny and I played with it until I came up with Nom Breakfast & Burgers."

All burgers are made with local beef and have a crusty exterior from being cooked on a flat top. They're served on buttered and toasted taro brioche buns, which are made by Passion Bakery in Kapaʻa. Dan likes The Woody with onion straws, cheddar cheese, bacon, jalapeños and barbecue sauce.

Chicken & Waffles with pineapple bourbon butter

"We get all of our beef from Mederios Farms in Kalāheo," says Thomas. "I think the meat has rich, flavorful quality."

Make sure to order a side of deep-fried tater tots, which evoke a gourmand childhood. Tot flavors have included garlic, white truffle, parsley and Parmesan; poutine; cheddar, sour cream and chives; and barbecue sauce, cheddar and bacon.

Chicken & Waffles is made with buttermilk and a hint of cinnamon, as well as a mixture of whole wheat and all-purpose flour. A buttermilk-fried chicken breast is served with chunky pineapple bourbon butter and maple syrup.

"We also make a vegan, gluten-free banana waffle that's to die for," says Thomas of the rice-based waffle made with mashed bananas and served with slices of fresh bananas, gluten-free granola and lilikoʻi syrup. "Every time we make it, the truck smells like freshly made banana bread."

Every Saturday, Thomas prepares 12 orders of flakey, scratch-made biscuits and tops them with white gravy studded with sausage and bacon.

"I render breakfast sausage and bacon and make a roux from the fat," explains Thomas. "I add heavy cream, whole milk, a lot of pepper and put all the meat back in. It's an homage to my grandmother who always made biscuits and gravy every weekend."

The Pineapple Martini has good looks and big flavor in the same glass

OASIS ON THE BEACH

Waipouli Beach Resort
4-820 Kūhiō Hwy., Kapaʻa
808-822-9332
www.OasisKauai.com
Farm to Table

Every time friends and family come for a visit, even if they're here for a just few days, we take them to Oasis. Tucked in the back of the Waipouli Beach Resort, the beachfront property offers breezy inside dining as well as a serene outdoor setting. The menu features local pork and grass-fed beef, fresh fish and Kauaʻi-grown produce.

Since opening in 2010, Oasis has been making positive contributions to the community. Managing Partner Stefan Mandel spearheads opportunities to support the island by using eco-friendly products such as flameless candles and buying 85 percent of his ingredients locally.

"It just makes sense," Stefan says. "When you buy locally, you use less fuel, less packaging, support local businesses, and the money stays on the island. We were ready when the plastic bag ban went into effect because we were already providing biodegradable bags and take-out containers."

We often see Stefan, as well as Executive Chef Sean Smull, at the Kapaʻa farmers market, their cart-on-wheels laden with fruit, vegetables and flowers.

The small menu is packed with mouthwatering selections and offers full plates and half portions. I always order organic East Coast mussels with ginger pork sausage and toast as well as the grilled kale salad with whipped Brie and pickled shallots. Dan, being the burger man, usually goes for the Makaweli Meat Co. grass-fed burger with crispy onions, bacon jam, arugula and chevre.

Cocktails suited to any palate are hand-crafted at Oasis on the Beach

The bar menu features unique, island-inspired cocktails, artisan beers and boutique wines. Take a seat at the custom-made canoe bar and enjoy happy hour, while the ocean breeze cools you down.

Sunday brunch features typical breakfast fare with a fresh, gourmet twist, including offerings such as Loco Moco with Cognac Gravy, Brisket Hash with Jalapeno Hollandaise and a breakfast wrap with eggs, bacon, spicy pepper aioli, Cheddar cheese and a farm fresh salad. There's someone playing slack key guitar, or ukulele during Sunday brunch and a special treat is when Aldrine Guerrero plays on Wednesday nights. He does a terrific rendition of Europa by Santana.

PACO'S TACOS HOUSE

4-1415 Kūhiō Hwy., Kapa'a
808-822-9944
www.pacostacoskauai.com
Mexican

BLD $$ 🌶 🍃 🌱 VEGAN 🌾

At Paco's Tacos House, Paco cooks while his brother, Tony, runs the front counter with a ready smile. Family photographs line the back wall and include the brothers' maternal grandpa, whose nickname was "El Chili Verde." In the center, their father and mother sit on a bench next the boy's favorite uncle and his wife. The final picture, on the far right, shows a gaggle of smiling kids. Nestled among the seven siblings are Tony (bottom right) and Paco (bottom left).

Tony and Paco Aguilar in front of Paco's Tacos House in Kapa'a

On the back counter, dual beverage dispensers chill and circulate house-made aguas frescas. Horchata, a traditional beverage made with ground rice, cinnamon and sugar, is always available. Aguas frescas are often made with seasonal fruit and today; the second circulator is filled with soursop.

"We grew up with this fruit in Ixtapa-Zihuatanejo," says Tony of his early years in the Mexican Riviera. "Soursop grows here so we decided to use it."

Tony says agua fresca means "refreshing beverage" and since opening, variations have included tamarind, watermelon, cantaloupe and hibiscus.

Paco's dishes, which are based on his family's recipes, were refined after the brothers worked at five-star hotels in Mexico.

"We always get fresh fish from local fishermen," Tony says, noting that specials depend on what is caught.

The Grilled Ono Taco features a juicy filet topped with shredded cabbage, pico de gallo and cilantro sauce. When you order, a basket filled with hot chips and a bowl of salsa fresca are delivered to your table, along with two squeeze bottles. One is filled with tangy tomatillo sauce and the other, a spicy chipotle crema that is so good; I squeeze it on every bite.

Tortillas are cooked to order and burritos are served plain; enchilada-style with red sauce and sour cream; smothered with pork chili verde; or chimichanga style, in which the burrito is fried and served with guacamole, lettuce, sour cream and pico de gallo.

Breakfast is available all day and the lengthy menu includes Paco Loco, with fried eggs, chili verde, rice and beans.

PANIOLO SANTA MARIA STYLE BBQ

4-1345 Kūhiō Hwy, Kapa'a
808-431-1668
facebook:Paniolo Grills Original Santa Maria Style BBQ
Santa Maria Style Barbecue

In 2014, the Diaz family introduced a 150-year-old California tradition to Kaua'i. Before then Art Diaz, his wife, Joanne, and their three children lived in Santa Maria, CA. The boys helped dad with his construction business and on Friday nights the family went to the Central City Farmers Market and danced, window-shopped and enjoyed legendary Santa Maria style barbecue.

The technique was invented in the Santa Maria Valley by vaqueros, or Mexican cowboys. They worked cattle ranches and owners gifted them off-cuts such as tritip. The vaqueros slow-cooked the meat over wood coals, transforming the tough meat into smoky succulence and creating a cult following.

In the early 90s, Art and Joanne moved to Kaua'i. Jared moved here in 2002, where he met and married Lenney. When the economy tanked in 2008, Art Jr. joined his family and they opened Recessions Original Santa Maria Style BBQ.

"It's our own style and something you can't find anywhere else on Kaua'i," Art Jr. explains. "We're not Texas barbecue. We're not Memphis barbecue. We have our own sweet style."

In Aug. 2016, they took over the former Holoholo Paniolo restaurant and changed the name to Paniolo Santa Maria Style BBQ. They still use a $10,000 custom made grill with wheels, which they take to events such as the Coconut Festival every October.

Oak and hickory coals smolder under the grill, which is topped with marinated tritip roasts, chicken breasts, French bread and a tray of sliced onions. Jared turns a handcranked wheel attached to heavy gauge chain and raises the grill top, enabling him to control the heat. Sliced open, the tri-tip has a nice pink smoke ring around the edges.

Art Jr. makes fresh salsa and chili con carne, which are traditional side dishes. Tri-tip Plates and Chicken Plates are served with chili over steamed rice, salsa and a green salad with

The Tri-tip sandwich will fill you up and put a smile on your face

tomatoes, feta cheese, dried cranberries and Italian dressing. Sandwiches are made with French bread, meat, caramelized onions and salsa. If you don't want bread, you can put all of that on a salad. As of this printing, new menu items were in the works, such as fresh island fish, burgers and Frito Pie.

69

PAPAYA'S NATURAL FOODS & CAFÉ

Kaua'i Village Shopping Center
4-831 Kūhiō Hwy. #330, Kapa'a
808-823-0190
www.PapayasNaturalFoods.com
Healthy Food

Papaya's is a long-standing, family-owned health food store. And with a name like "Papaya's" they had to sell papayas. GMO-free advocates frequent health food stores and many eliminate papayas from their diet. That's because most of the papayas sold in Hawai'i are genetically modified to resist Papaya Ringspot Virus. Owner Jessica Leech has local farmers send leaf samples to the University of Hawai'i for testing. If they come back clean, the papayas get put in the produce section along with a wide variety of local and/or organic produce.

Dietary concerns are carefully considered before a meal is prepared in the grocery store's small café. The chefs—who avoid using known allergens—cook meals that are low in fat, salt and/or sugar. Ingredients are minimally processed, pesticide free, not genetically modified and meat is from antibiotic-free animals that are raised under humane conditions. It doesn't matter if you're lactose free, gluten free, vegan, raw, vegetarian or a food-a-tarian: you can enjoy tasty and wholesome food at the café.

The salad bar is loaded with 32 local and/or organic items, such as produce, tofu, beans and five types of dressing. A hot bar offers breakfast burritos, marinated and grilled tofu, brown rice, sesame onion tofu sauce, soup of the day, tofu musubi with brown rice and furikake and breakfast burritos. The salad bar and hot bar are both vegetarian.

Coconuts can be bought in the produce section and cracked open at the café, which also serves fresh juice and noni or wheatgrass shots. The Chai Chai Chia smoothie is made with local bananas, Tipu's micro ground chai (also available in bags of loose tea), chia seeds, coconut milk, SPIRU-TEIN protein powder and your choice of soy or rice milk. Since this smoothie is so filling, delicious and full of caffeine, it makes a wonderful lunch or afternoon pick-me-up.

Owner Jessica Leech with her sons, Eli and Zeb

Meals include popular fish tacos on organic corn or flour tortillas with vegetable slaw, cilantro cream, or chipotle aioli (mayonnaise). For the Blackened Fish Nori Wrap, nori is placed on a flour tortilla along with brown rice, lettuce, tomatoes and fresh fish coated with Cajun seasoning.

"People think our only customers are hippies, but all types of professionals come here," Jessica says. "With startling rates of obesity and disease, everyone can benefit from making a simple change in their life."

PASSION BAKERY & CAFÉ

4-356 Kūhiō Hwy., Kapaʻa
808-821-0060
www.KinipopoVillage.com/passion_bakery.htm
Bakery

BL $ 🥥 🌿 VEGAN 🚫🌾

For 15 years, Michael Sterioff flew to Italy and sold automotive gauges to high-volume manufacturers. It was during these trips that a romance with Italian bread rose like soft balls of dough and left him smoldering, long after he returned to his home in Michigan.

"When I ate focaccia at a friend's house, it was the most amazing flavor of my life," Sterioff says, recalling a long-ago dinner in Italy. "I never enjoyed bread until that night, and by the end of the evening, he gave me the recipe."

By the time Sterioff mastered that recipe, he taught himself how to make sourdough. An artisan bakery opened near his office, and he worked there on the weekends for free. After eight months, he developed a signature line of breads.

Sterioff and his wife, Magda, opened Passion Bakery in April 2010. Organic flour is used to make pillowy soft taro brioche rolls, crusty whole-wheat loaves, rosemary focaccia and sourdough from a house-made starter.

A glass case holds baked goods such as cheesecake-filled muffins made with local passion fruit, Key limes and mangos. Apple bananas are used in the walnut-banana bread, and gluten-free

Michael Sterioff is the owner of Passion Bakery

cinnamon-pecan and coconut cream coffeecake offer alternative choices. Vegan cookies made with almond meal, roasted hazelnuts, rosemary and Alaea sea salt are a delicious combination of sweet and salty.

Hot breakfast "eggwiches" feature thick frittatas made with meat and cheese sandwiched between slices of freshly baked croissants, taro brioche buns, sourdough or whole wheat bread. Lunch includes turkey, ham, salami or roast beef sandwiches and daily specials. House-made chai tea and espresso is also served. Seating is limited and parking is tricky.

SCORPACCIATA

4-1306 Kūhiō Hwy, Kapa'a
808-635-5569
Instagram: scorpacciatakauai
Italian

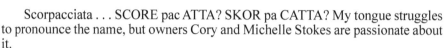

Scorpacciata . . . SCORE pac ATTA? SKOR pa CATTA? My tongue struggles to pronounce the name, but owners Cory and Michelle Stokes are passionate about it.

"Score POTCH chee yatta," Michelle says. "It's Italian and means to eat a big feast of what's local and in season."

Okay!

Michelle and I chat at a picnic table in front of their food truck. Scorpacciata specializes in Neapolitan pizza, which is made in an 800-degree oven in 90 seconds. Two young ladies sit next to us and enjoy a breakfast pizza made with potatoes, an egg, maple syrup and Millionaire's Bacon, which is baked with ground chili peppers and maple syrup. Michelle, a petite mother of five, wears her short black hair tucked into a grey knit cap while their daughter, Samantha, helps her dad cook.

Cory trained under Jean Marie Josselin at A Pacific Cafe in Kapa'a before cooking at Tidepools and Dondero's, two restaurants at the Grand Hyatt Kaua'i Resort & Spa. Today, he is a personal chef and uses ingredients from his family's organic garden.

Pizza specials have featured Da Mango with mango jam from My Kaua'i Honey Co., prosciutto, fresh basil, goat cheese and fresh mozzarella drizzled with a

Creamy polenta with house-made marinara topped with a fried egg is a great way to start the day

balsamic reduction; roasted shiitake and oyster mushrooms from Lāwa'i Valley, pesto, fresh mozzarella, arugula and truffle oil; and the Fig n' Pig with kālua pork, fig jam, basil and a drizzle of reduced balsamic vinegar. Vegan pizza is made with eggplant, tomatoes, caramelized onions, basil and a balsamic reduction.

The breakfast sandwich includes soft bread filled with crisp arugula, a fried egg, thinly sliced potatoes that are crunchy on the outside and soft on the inside, and Millionaire's Bacon. Breakfast specials have included creamy polenta with marinara, a fried egg and Parmesan shavings; banana buckwheat pancakes with caramelized apple bananas, rum butter, maple syrup and whipped cream; and whole wheat French toast with blueberry syrup and fresh whipped cream.

SHAVE ICE TEGE TEGE

4-1604 Kūhiō Hwy., Kapaʻa
Just North of Otsuka's Furniture
www.ShaveIceTegeTege.com
Shave Ice

Shave ice is typically made from thin shavings of ice and syrup, which is made with high fructose corn syrup, artificial flavorings and food coloring. At Shave Ice Tege Tege, all syrups and ice creams are handmade with whole fruit and 100 percent organic ingredients.

Owner Eiataro (pronounced "Aye ta roe") Hisahara is from Amami, a group of islands in Japan near Okinawa, where "tege tege" is slang for "just right." Shave ice is extremely popular there and making it with a hand-cranked Hatsuyuki Ice Shaver is essential.

Organic green tea ice cream with azuki bean paste

A unique blade gives Eiataro total control and his shave ice is like freshly fallen snow. He tops it with thick syrup made with berries or seasonal fruit from the farmers market. Before adding fruit, Eiataro begins by making two syrup bases: one from cane sugar and the other with local honey.

Seasonal flavors include lemon, pineapple, mango and lilikoʻi (passion fruit). Other offerings include blueberry, blackberry, coconut, brown sugar and green tea.

"Japanese people have a refined palate," explains Sumi, Eiataro's wife. "He's very particular with his syrups and how he makes the shave ice taste. He'll test a recipe for a month or two to make it perfect."

Azuki bean paste, a common option for shave ice, originated in China where there are two preparations. Koshian, a smooth paste that's been passed through a sieve, is the typical addition to shave ice. Tsubuan are beans that have been left whole. Eiataro uses both types and starts by slow cooking azuki beans in cane sugar. He purees most of them, but every bite or so, you'll find a whole bean.

My favorite is the Japanese Green Tea with azuki beans. Layers of "snow" alternate with green tea syrup. Organic condensed milk is drizzled on top, along with a scoop of green tea ice cream (also made by Eiataro) and more azuki bean paste.

SHIVALIK INDIAN CUISINE

Waipouli Shopping Center
4771 Kūhiō Hwy., Kapa'a
808-821-2333
www.ShivalikIndianCuisine.com
Indian

Indian music softly plays in the background and warm spices scent the air at Shivalik Indian Cuisine. There is light, jovial conversation as customers enjoy dinner at Kaua'i's only full service Indian restaurant. Shivalik (pronounced "She vah lick") means a gathering place. For Hindus, Shiva is the Lord of mercy and compassion, and when you sit together for a meal the place is called Shivalik.

When owner Sam Sudhakaran reopened under new management in April 2014, he hired a new crew including a curry chef, a tandoor chef and two prep chefs.

Thali, "a traditional Indian take on the classic plate lunch," includes a main entrée, basmati rice, yellow dal, vegetable curry, achar (Indian pickle), naan and salad. As of this writing, Sam plans to add dosas, a south Indian "pancake" that is large, thin and made with ground rice and lentils.

Vegetarian entrées range from Paneer Makhni (fresh-made Indian cheese cooked in a rich tomato sauce) and Chana Masala (garbanzo beans slowly cooked in an onion sauce), to Malai Kofta (vegetable dumplings simmered in a creamy sauce) and Baingan Bhartha (tandoor roasted eggplant in a rich herb and spice mixture).

Curries are like a flavorful stew, full of aromatic spices, but vary in contents. The curry chef makes three sauce bases—tomato, onion and cashew—and expertly blends them with lamb, beef, fish or chicken.

Vegetable samosas are filled with potatoes, wrapped in a light and flaky pastry and deep-fried. Jeera Chawal, India's prized basmati rice is steamed and lightly spiced. Nimbu Chawal includes turmeric-stained basmati rice flavored with fresh lemon juice and flecked with toasted nuts and mustard seeds. Naan, which is baked to order in the Tandoor oven, is soft, chewy and addictive. Lassan Naan is spread with freshly minced garlic and cilantro.

At Shivalik Indian Cuisine, the Lassan Naan is brushed with garlic and cilantro before baking

They'll ask how hot you want your meal, as in spicy not temperature. Daniel's favorite is Vindaloo, which is made with cumin, onion, tomato and chili peppers and is the hottest preparation they have!

SMALL TOWN COFFEE

The big red bus at
4-1543 Kūhiō Hwy., Kapaʻa
808-821-1604
www.SmallTownCoffee.com
Coffee Shop

In September 2014, Small Town Coffee moved from the Kauaʻi Crafts Fair into a big red bus in the Kojima's Shopping center, about three blocks south. Award-winning fair-trade beans from Barefoot Coffee Roasters in California are freshly ground for espresso. The daily brew is made from a custom blend by Kauaʻi Roastery in Waimea, who specializes in coffee from farms that meet sustainable agronomic practices.

The coffee is tasty and beautiful

"Richard Loero roasts it the way I want," says co-owner Anni Caporuscio of her house blend that contains 30 percent Kaʻu coffee from the Big Island. The remaining 70 percent is a blend of Peruvian and Nicaraguan beans. "I like mildly roasted coffees. Many roasters of Hawaiian coffee roast it too darkly, so you're not getting the intricacies of what Hawaiʻi beans are.

"Hawaiʻi beans are lighter, nuttier, and make a thinner bodied coffee. It's brighter. It's more on the top of your mouth."

Anni's had a liquid fascination since childhood. At the age of three, she made pretty designs in her glass of milk. Today, the award-winning barista makes latte art.

"You know how people say they're foodies?" Anni asks. "I'm a liquid person. But there's really no way to say that. I'm liquidic?"

Sunset Magazine is impressed with her fluid flair, and the Spring 2011 issue declared that Small Town Coffee served "quite possibly the best lattes in the world." Anni won the Big Island barista competitions in 2006 and 2007. "To win, you have to do it quickly, cleanly and it has to taste good. You have to talk while you do it, and make it pretty with latte art," she explained.

A variety of scones, muffins and are made daily and include regular, gluten-free and vegan options. Coffee syrups are made in-house.

STREET BURGER

4-369 Kūhiō Hwy., Kapa'a
808-212-1555
www.streetburgerkauai.com
Burgers

With wood panels, tin siding and air-conditioning, Street Burger is an upscale yet rustic restaurant. Owners Kristen and Aaron Leikam (a husband and wife team who formally owned Cakes by Kristen) opened in Sept. 2015. There is ample parking in the back and smoke clings to the outside air, giving a hint of what's inside. The gourmet burger bar seats about 60, and there are 24 beers, two hard ciders and two wines on tap. Customers can sit at stainless-steel topped tables in the dining area, outdoors on a covered lanai, on stools at the beer bar, or at the Chef's Counter.

Aaron stands at the wood-fire grill, squinting from the smoke of burning kiawe, guava, ironwood and lychee. He raises and lowers an iron grate that is suspended over the coals by turning a steel wheel. The grate is loaded with 6-ounce patties made of grass fed beef from Makaweli Meat Co., a ranch on Kaua'i's West Side.

All burgers are served on a taro brioche bun made by Passion Bakery in Kapa'a. There are five "classic" burgers and 12 exotic burgers including the Farmer with tomato jam, grilled onions, aged Gouda cheese, arugula and a fried egg.

Everything is made in-house, including mustard, mayonnaise, ketchup, French fries and pork belly. There are six types of specialty fries, including herbed, truffle

The dining room at Street Burger has a rustic and comfortable feel

There are 24 beers on tap at Street Burger, more than any other bar on the island

and garlic and Texas poutine with chili, sharp cheddar, poached egg and onions. Substitutions are "politely declined" and all burger orders come with sea salt fries. If you want one of the specialty fries, you have to order it on the side and eat two sets of fries.

'Ahi crudo includes cubes of fresh 'ahi blended with olive oil, oranges that have been caramelized on the grill, Maui onions and green Sicilian olives. Bottarga--which is Mediterranean salted, cured tuna roe--is shaved on top. Five entrée salads include the Street Salad with kale, peppadews, Gouda, pork belly, poached egg and lemon vinaigrette; and duck confit with arugula, onions, Manchego cheese, capers and caramelized oranges.

Kristen makes desserts, which typically include the Macadamia Honey Tart, which is topped with freshly whipped cream and a swirl of dark chocolate sauce; and the Street Burger S'more, with peanut butter feuilletine (crispy pastry flakes), chocolate mousse and house-made marshmallow fluff.

DRINK LUXURIOUSLY

ANNI CAPORUSCIO, CO-OWNER OF SMALL TOWN COFFEE, THINKS THAT EVERYONE SHOULD DO IT RIGHT AND TAKE A LITTLE EXTRA TIME TO DRINK THEIR NUTRITION. MARINATE, STORE, INFUSE, BLEND, MIX, MUDDLE. DO ANYTHING TO AVOID THE ARTIFICIAL TASTE LEFT IN YOUR MOUTH FROM POWDERED MILK, PRESERVATIVES, SWEETENERS, ARTIFICIAL FLAVORS AND OVERLY SWEET MIXERS. SHE SAYS IF YOU'RE GOING TO DRINK LUXURIES, DRINK LUXURIOUSLY.

TIKI TACOS

4-961 Kūhiō Hwy., Kapa'a
808-823-TACO (8226)
www.Facebook.com/TikiTacos
Mexican

Hilda Morales makes one damn fine taco. It's messy for sure: loaded with moist, chunky meat, charred and smoky from the grill, and depending on what you get, gobs of guacamole, cabbage, chili peppers or tomatoes. Tortillas are made from scratch, including yellow corn and the organic, GMO-free blue corn. If you don't want a tortilla, you can order a salad of local greens topped with taco fillings.

Eat local at Tiki Tacos

The tacos are perfection, and maybe that's because tacos are their specialty. You won't find enchiladas, burritos, or fajitas. Saturday is the only day you can get tamales, and look for soup specials such as posole and menudo.

"Our concept is to be an authentic taqueria," says Morales, who was born and raised in Acapulco, Mexico, and moved to Kaua'i 18 years ago. "That means only tacos and no fillers like rice, beans or chips."

Morales runs the small restaurant with her husband, Bard Widmer. And when Tiki Tacos says it's spicy, they're not kidding. The medium salsa may be rated as "burn your face off" by some, but it's perfect for me. Chilies find their way into everything, including chunks of serrano in the Tiki Fire Asada Beef Taco.

With a mother who worked full time, Morales spent her childhood with her grandmother who owned and operated a restaurant and used ingredients grown on her farm. Her grandmother's twin sister would come with fresh fish, crab, corn and other vegetables, and Morales watched them make tortillas and cook.

Morales says 95 percent of her ingredients come from Hawai'i and she tries to source from Kaua'i first. They only serve 100 percent Kaua'i-grown beef and lamb, and when those aren't available, they're not on the menu.

"I want to support our local economy," says Morales. "So, when they have it, we have it. When they don't, we don't. Some people don't understand, but I'm not going to buy lamb from New Zealand when I can get it here."

"It's difficult and challenging to support the island," she continues. "The island is a very fragile environment. If we start ordering from other places, the economy will suffer, and the small businesses here will suffer."

VERDE

4-1101 Kūhiō Hwy, A-3, Kapaʻa
808-821-1400
www.VerdeHawaii.com
New Mexican

Verde, a beloved New Mexican restaurant located in Kapaʻa, recently infused its menu with "clean" ingredients, including produce that was grown on Kauaʻi, as well as antibiotic free chicken and pork. From the beginning, they've served Kailani Farms' lettuce mix and for the past two years, grass-fed beef from Makaweli Meat Co., located on Kauaʻi's West Side. Buying precut vegetables in large quantities streamlines work in the kitchen, so Verde's choice to serve locally grown food is labor intensive.

For owner Maris Manzano, creating food security means partnering with local businesses. Spirit of the Earth, a biodynamic farm located in Moloaʻa, grows cilantro and sweet potato greens. Spinach, which does not grow well on Kauaʻi, has been replaced with sweet potato greens, which thrive here with minimal effort. They are rich in vitamin B, beta carotene, iron, calcium, zinc and protein and after a quick sauté; they have a mild taste and rich body.

Moloaʻa Organicaʻa, a certified organic farm in Moloaʻa, supplies long beans, which are a simple replacement for imported green beans. Linda Yoshii, who also grows in Moloaʻa, provides avocados and Tahitian limes.

Verde partnered with Kauaʻi Juice Co., for their Pina Verde Picante margarita, a blend of fresh pineapple, lemon and fermented chili peppers with muddled cilantro, organic tequila and Grand Marnier.

Dan's favorite is the Carne Adovada "Red Pork" Burrito with potatoes and cheese. I prefer the Bean and Cheese Tostada, with house-made refried beans, green sauce, a pile of Kailani greens, guacamole, garlic aioli and chipotle sauce. 'Ahi Tacos are made with fresh, Hawaiian tuna that is seared rare, topped with shredded cabbage, fresh-made guacamole, pico de gallo, tortilla strips and garlic aioli. My Kauaʻi Honey is served with plain sopaipillas and blended with butter and served as a dip with Churro Fries.

While purchasing from local farmers costs more, which is reflected in the prices, we are grateful that Verde makes it easy to increase food security on Kauaʻi. Maris is planning on opening a second location in Līhuʻe at Hokulei Village.

The food at Verde is packed with flavor

WAILUĀ SHAVE ICE

4-1306 Kūhiō Hwy, Kapa'a
808-634-7183
www.wailuashaveice.com
Shave Ice

Wailuā Shave Ice owners Josh Tamaoka and Brandon Baptiste have re-imagined a Hawaiian tradition. House-made syrups containing organic cane sugar, local fruit, and coffee, replace the typical kind, which is leaden with high fructose corn syrup, artificial colors and preserves.

Josh and Brandon were born and raised on Kaua'i, in the town of Wailuā. After Brandon graduated culinary school, he worked across the country before cooking at Per Se, Thomas Keller's renowned restaurant in New York. He was homesick and decided to partner with his childhood buddy, Josh, and open a simple place that serves quality shave ice with generous helpings of old fashioned aloha.

Their food truck, which is more like a wagon, is tucked in a grassy alley near Pono Market. A steady stream of customers enjoys tropical treats at nearby picnic tables that are covered with umbrellas. Other patrons sit on barstools lining either side of the wagon.

"We learned how to make shave ice from uncle near Big Save," says Brandon as he loads a cylinder of ice into a machine. "He's been doing it since I was born, literally. He taught us how to make the perfect block of ice so it shaves up light and fluffy."

Downy ice is piled into white pyrex bowls and syrup is drizzled over the top. "Coconut x Coconut x Coconut" is rich with coconut milk, thick coconut sauce and roasted coconut flakes. Ginger Ale is made with lemon and lime syrup and chunks of candied ginger. "Small Kine" Mocha, made with beans roasted at Small Kine Coffee, has coconut foam drizzled over the ice followed by a dusting of cacao powder.

The menu changes with the seasons, but other popular flavors have included Kaua'i Dream (orange, vanilla and ginger), Pineapple Pickers (pineapple and vanilla bean), Banana Horchata (horchata, bananas and cinnamon) and Love Potion #9 (vanilla bean milk, strawberry puree and fresh cut strawberries)

Wailua Shave Ice is a perfect way to cool off

When you have their shave ice in hand, you can't help but break into a big smile

CENTRAL

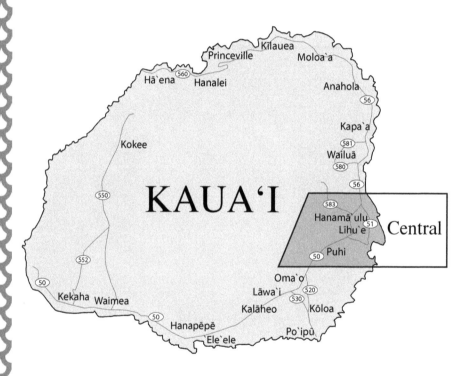

The majestic Wailua Falls

BAMBOO GRILL & SUSHI

Anchor Cove Shopping Center
3416 Rice St., Līhu'e
808-245-6886
www.BambooGrillAndSushiKauai.com
Japanese, American and Hawaiian

Bamboo Grill & Sushi is located along Kalapaki Bay, and if you sit in the small, outside dining area you have a view of the ocean. Inside the huge dining area, there's a full bar. The dinner menu features sushi, bento boxes, noodle dishes as well as meat, fish and seafood entrées. We love the deep-fried Spicy Korean Chicken Bites, which can be ordered with a side of brown rice and a fresh salad if you want to be a little bit healthy.

Richie Ogata, the easy-going owner, sometimes mixes drinks and talks story behind the bar. He credits his mother for his entrepreneurial spirit and praises her cooking skills.

"The Oki Pancakes are my mom's recipe," says Ogata of Barbara Oki, former owner of the now-closed Oki Diner. "I'm not really a pancake eater but after trying her pancakes I can see why people like them so much! Usually some places you gonna eat pancakes, they're heavy, kinda doughy. These ones are real nice, light, fluffy!"

Pancakes are topped with his mother's thick coconut syrup. After two years of recipe development, she made a powder form (www.kauaitropicalsyrup.com), which can also be made into haupia, coconut tapioca pudding or rice pudding. I bought some at Safeway and it was coconuty, creamy and very easy to make.

Ogata's sushi is also popular. My favorite is the Eternal Sunshine, which is beautifully presented and filled with tempura shrimp and avocado. Succulent salmon slices are draped over the roll and topped with thin slices of lemon. Ogata also serves, in my opinion, the best saimin on Kaua'i.

GIVE FISH A CHANCE

IF RAW FISH (OR FISH IN GENERAL) MAKES YOU SQUEAMISH, IT'S LIKELY BECAUSE YOU'RE FROM A LAND-LOCKED AREA WHERE FRESH FISH IS ABOUT AS LIKELY AS SNOW FALLING ON KAUA'I. I'M ORIGINALLY FROM COLORADO AND I HAVE BEEN BLASTED BY THE SMELL OF THE FISH DEPARTMENT AS SOON AS I'VE WALKED INTO A GROCERY STORE. IN HAWAI'I, THE FISH ARE SUPER FRESH, THEIR JUICY FLESH IS SWEET AND THEIR FRAGRANCE IS LIKE THE BRINY BREEZE OF THE OCEAN. DO YOURSELF A FAVOR AND TRY 'AHI POKĒ AND COOKED FISH AT LEAST ONCE.

CULINARY ARTS PROGRAM

Kaua'i Community College
3-1901 Kaumuali'i Hwy., Līhu'e
808-245-8365
Continental Cuisine, Asian Cuisine

Three days a week during the academic year, second-year students at the Kaua'i Community College Culinary Arts Program put their skills to practice, and people can enjoy a fine-dining experience at budget-friendly prices.

Every spring, students cook a multi-course meal in the college's Fine Dining Restaurant. Hawaiian music softly plays in the air-conditioned dining room and oversized windows frame emerald mountains and an indigo sky. White tablecloths are topped with blushing anthuriums and polished silverware. Instructor Duane Miyasato quietly escorts guests to their table, pulls out their chair and, with a graceful flick of the wrist, presents them with a red linen napkin.

For six of the weeks, students make continental cuisine featuring American and European classics such as French Onion Soup, Chicken Chasseur with

Marinated beef on a bed of oranges

potato pancakes, and rib eye with au jus. The remaining six weeks are dedicated to different regions of Asia. Diners enjoy traditional dishes from Japan, Thailand, Vietnam, Korea, the Pacific Islands, and China, including the Sìchuān province.

"Our sole purpose is to ready students for the work force," explains Assistant Professor Martina Hilldorfer. "We have a board of advisors and an employer focus group, and we groom our students to industry standards."

Lunch is popular with Kaua'i residents because for a nominal price, you get a lot of delicious food. The menu changes every week but you always get rolls, choice of an appetizer or salad, choice of a main dish, and choice of dessert. There are usually two to three options in each category. The students are sharpening their culinary skills so the staff asks that guests not make special requests. Reservations are a must.

DANI'S RESTAURANT

4201 Rice St., Līhu'e
808-245-4991
www.facebook.com/Danis-Restaurant-144708642278853
Japanese, American and Hawaiian

Dani's Restaurant is built on hard work that goes back four generations. In 1964, Akiyo Honjo opened her restaurant Ma's Place—which was just up from Dani's on Rice Street—and worked there until she was 94 years old. Her daughter, Harriet, married Tsutao Morioka, and the couple opened Dani's Restaurant in 1981.

"My parents decided to name it after me," says Danny Morioka, who was 8 years old when the restaurant opened. "They didn't want spell it Danny because it would be too close to Denny's, so they came up with this variation."

Growing up in a restaurant environment inspired Danny to cook. After attending Kaua'i Community College and Kapi'olani Community College on O'ahu, he worked with Jean Marie Josselin and D.K. Kodama, who owns d.k. Sean as well as Sansei Seafood Restaurant & Sushi Bar on O'ahu.

When Danny and his wife, Julie, returned to Kaua'i in 2006, they assumed responsibility for Dani's. They are slowly making changes, such as printing a new version of the 33-year-old menu, while honoring the older generation who likes things just the way they are.

The Bacon Cheeseburger Loco Moco, listed on the menu as B.C.L.M., is a newer menu item. Fresh ground beef hand-shaped into a large oval patty is placed on a mound of steamed white rice. Pan drippings from roast pork go into the gravy, which smothers two eggs. American cheese, crisp bacon crumbles and thinly sliced scallions are sprinkled on top.

The B.C.L.M.: Bacon Cheeseburger Loco Moco

Everything on the Lū'au Plate is made from scratch, including a hefty serving of tender pork that's wrapped in taro leaves, which were grown in Hanalei. Dani's version of pipikaula features red chili flakes that cling to juicy cubes of tender beef. Their succulent kālua pig has a good balance of salt and smoke. The dish comes with a side of fresh poi, a small bowl of lomi salmon and two scoops of white or brown rice.

Danny's sauces, named "Flavors of Kaua'i," were invented when he and his wife tried to get their young daughters to eat vegetables. Flavor-Burst, a sesame and shoyu blend and Miso Marinade are available for purchase at the restaurant. Recipes provided if you ask!

GAYLORD'S

Kilohana Plantation
3-2087 Kaumuali'i Hwy., Līhu'e
808-245-5608
www.GaylordsKauai.com
Hawai'i Regional Cuisine

Gaylord's restaurant is located at Kilohana Plantation inside the historic Wilcox Mansion, a 16,000-square-foot Tudor-style house built in English country house tradition. There is outside dining and a narrow roof protects you from sun. Tables face the courtyard—available for live music and dancing—and views of the tropical landscaping beyond. In 2013, Kilohana Plantation renovated Wilcox Mansion's living room into the Mahiko Lounge, which includes a handcrafted, solid teak bar that seats 16. The combination of friendly service, serene atmosphere and delicious food encourages you to unwind and live the good life. Many of the restaurant's ingredients are harvested from onsite gardens and orchards.

Lunch includes beer-battered Fish Tacos; Kilohana Cobb Salad; and Red Wine Braised Beef Short-rib "Dip" served with horseradish whipped cream, Gruyère, toasted sourdough baguette, French onion au jus and onion rings.

Dinner includes fresh fish poached in extra virgin olive oil with lemon herb risotto or pork osso bucco with potato parsnip purée. Kiawe (mesquite) smoked prime rib, which is also available blackened, is served on Friday and Saturday nights.

Whether it's lunch or dinner, save room for the Classic Banana Coconut Cream Pie. The crust is gluten-free, which doesn't matter to me, but the pie is not to be missed! Apple bananas, which are grown on the property, are folded into a creamy custard. The pie is topped

Outdoor dining around the couryard at Gaylord's

with Kōloa Rum Kaua'i Gold whipped cream, toasted coconut, butterscotch sauce and candied walnuts.

Sunday brunch includes a selection of gourmet breakfast items such as seared 'ahi Benedict with wasabi hollandaise. For a little extra, you can drink all the champagne or mimosas you want.

THE GREENERY CAFÉ

3146 Akahi St., Līhuʻe
808-635-2752
www.TheGreeneryCafe.com
Southern & Soul Food

The Greenery Café serves wholesome comfort food with Southern, Filipino and Hawaiian influences. Dayne Greene and his wife, Neina, have a kindred affection for food and were inspired to open their café in Līhuʻe. Southern influences are inspired by Dayne's family, who are from North Carolina and Alabama, and Neina adds the Filipino flair.

Tucked inside a plantation-style building, pale yellow walls with sea foam green trim surround the outside dining area, which is covered. A hand-painted sign reads "Organic Soul Food. Farm 2 Table. Coffee. Teas." Around back, a garden with rosemary, thyme, chives and parsley supplies the kitchen with fresh herbs.

In 1995, Dayne, a graduate of Tuskegee University, was living in Washington, D.C., when he lost the use of his legs in a random shooting. While recovering, he became hyper-aware of his food choices and extra cautious about the foods he ate.

"Nowadays, it's especially important for us to pick and choose our ingredients," explains Dayne. "Because in our country, our food is tampered with a lot more than it needs to be and it wasn't like that in my grandma's day."

Eating at the Greenery Café feels like you are having a home-cooked meal

A glass of fresh watermelon juice blended with rice milk is a sweet pairing to the signature Rosemary Chicken Plate, which comes with a choice of two sides, including sweet potato yams, collard greens, garden salad, potato salad, coleslaw, black-eyed peas, rice or quinoa.

Dayne marinates organic chicken breasts overnight in fresh rosemary, pepper sauce, garlic and cracked pepper. He cooks it low and slow and expertly coaxes it into succulence. His vegan collard green recipe includes bell peppers, tomatoes and garlic. Yams are roasted with cinnamon, brown sugar and local honey.

Neina puts a Hawaiian twist on binignit, a traditional Filipino rice pudding. Her lightly sweetened version, which is served warm and soupy, includes soft chunks of taro, mango, banana and sweet potatoes.

"For me, it's like going back to my roots and the essence of the food," Dayne says. "It's about getting pure food without the unnecessary preservatives or additives. Plus, I believe it tastes better!"

Rosemary Chicken Plate

WHAT IS LOCAL FOOD?

PEOPLE OFTEN ASK ME, "WHERE CAN I GET GOOD, LOCAL FOOD?" THAT DEPENDS ON THE TYPE OF LOCAL FOOD YOU WANT.

LOCAL FOOD CAN MEAN TRADITIONAL HAWAIIAN FOOD, WHICH INCLUDES LAULAU, POKĒ, KĀLUA PORK, POI, HAUPIA, AND KŪLOLO.

LOCAL FOOD CAN ALSO MEAN PLANTATION-ERA FOOD, WHICH WAS BROUGHT BY CULTURES WHO IMMIGRATED TO HAWAI'I TO WORK IN SUGAR OR PINEAPPLE FIELDS. "PLANTATION FOOD" IS A BLEND OF CULTURES FROM COUNTRIES SUCH AS CHINA, JAPAN, OKINAWA, KOREA, PHILIPPINES, AMERICA, PUERTO RICO AND PORTUGAL. DISHES INCLUDE CHICKEN HEKKA, CHICKEN KATSU, LOCO MOCO, KALBI SHORT RIBS, SPAM® MUSUBI, MANAPUA, MALASADAS, SAIMIN, TERIYAKI CHICKEN AND BEEF STEW.

LOCAL FOOD CAN ALSO MEAN FOOD THAT WAS GROWN, RAISED OR MADE HERE, AND OFTEN TRANSLATES TO HAWAII REGIONAL CUISINE.

HĀ COFFEE BAR

4180 Rice Street, Līhuʻe
808-631-9241
www.HaCoffeeBar.com
Coffee Shop

There's a calm urgency inside Hā Coffee Bar. A vaulted ceiling with lazy fans and an uncluttered floor give a sense of peaceful openness. Baristas quietly pull espressos and cloud workers sit in front of laptops, using free WiFi to get in a day of work. Merchandise is stacked on a shelf, near a play area for children, which is empty at the moment. Contemporary music muffles the discussions of local politicians, who meet over a cup of coffee.

Good coffee and good people

"We are set up to annunciate the idea of hā," says Jeff Adams, a Christian pastor for Seaside Church and executive director of the non-profit Seaside Kauaʻi, which does business as Hā Coffee Bar. "How do you breathe life into the community? We love Jesus and we want to love our neighbors. Instead of moving in and starting a church community, we asked, 'What would it look like if we came in and really loved the community?'"

One way Hā Coffee decided to do that is by supporting local businesses, such as bakeries, roasters and growers, by giving them the space to grow.

Kombucha from Kauaʻi Juice Co. is on tap. Kauaʻi Roastery roasts coffee beans, and blends include beans from the Kau region of Hawaiʻi Island, organic beans from Papua New Guinea and Bali Blue Moon, an organic blend with citrus notes.

Local vendors make baked goods such as banana bread and brownies from Keoki's, cookies from Aloha Sweet Delites and scones from Mailani Sweet Treats.

Three açaí bowls offer a different combination of coconut milk, soy milk, raw cacao nibs, hemp hearts (raw, shelled hemp seeds), granola, raw Kauaʻi honey, peanut butter, shredded coconut, sliced bananas, bee pollen, dark chocolate chips and chia seeds.

There are more than 20 types of tea, including two from Kauaʻi Farmacy, which grows organic herbs on the North Shore and blends them into medicinal teas. Tranquility Tea has a calming effect with gardenia and valerian. Energy tea, with ashwagandha and gotu kola, lives up to its name and I feel energized shortly after I drink it.

"We don't want people to think, 'This is a Christian coffee shop,' or 'This is a non-profit coffee shop,'" says Jeff. "We want people to come in and think, 'This is a really great coffee shop.'"

JC's Puerto Rican Kitchen

Kaua'i Community Farmers Market
808-652-5309
www.Facebook.com/JcsPuertoRicanTacos
Puerto Rican and Hawaiian

"I grew up in the kitchen watching my grandmother and father cook," recalls John Cabello. "The pan I use today to make my empanadas is the same one my father used when he taught me how to make them. Those kind of memories are infused in my heart and in my soul and in my love of cooking."

John and Rhonda Cabello, owners of JC's Puerto Rican Kitchen, cater events and set up a booth at the Saturday farmers market at the Kaua'i Community College in Līhu'e. They specialize in tacos, burritos and Arroz con Gandules, or rice with pigeon peas, locally pronounced as "gan du dee."

"It all starts with a sofrito," says John. "Every Puerto Rican family who loves to cook has a base flavor, and that comes from the sofrito. So the beef, chicken and rice are cooked in that."

John is a senior pastor at New Hope Christian Fellowship in Līhu'e where Rhonda heads up the Hula Hālau Dance Team. The "JC" in JC's Puerto Rican Kitchen stands for Jesus Christ, and the couple weaves love and aloha into their food.

"For me, food has always been a staple. I used to be in the Marine Corps, and I always ate with people I didn't know. As a pastor, when I look at the gospel, Jesus is always eating, always having a good time. Food does that for people," John says. "When we serve our food, we like to give people encouragement and lift them up."

Rhonda is a blend of Hawaiian, Chinese, Filipino and Portuguese. Growing up, she and her mother lived in the old Kealia Camp. Rhonda uses her grandmother's recipe for pasteles—a Portuguese "tamale" that uses green bananas instead of corn.

Most meals come with taro salad, which replaces the traditional mac salad, and a scoop of gandule rice, which replaces Hawai'i's ubiquitous steamed white rice.

Noah, Rhonda, John, Elijah and Jonah Cabello

KALAPAKI JOE'S

Kukui Grove Center
3-2600 Kaumuali'i Hwy, Līhu'e
808-245-6266
www.KalapakiJoes.com
American and Hawaiian

Though Kalapaki Joe's closed its original location on the upper level of the Harbor Mall, as well as its third location at the historic Waimea Plantation Cottages, its second location in Po'ipū and fourth, at Kukui Grove Shopping Center, are still open.

An extensive menu includes typical bar food: mozzarella sticks, wings, deep-fried calamari, tacos, burgers and beer-battered fish. But if you look closer, you'll find fresh food as well.

'Ahi Avocado Poke is made with fresh Hawaiian tuna, sesame oil, soy sauce and chili pepper flakes, slivers of onion and chunks of avocado. Pesto Glazed Local Fish comes with steamed rice and a garden salad. Vegetarian options include Fresh Portobello Enchiladas with homemade salsa rojo and we especially like the cocktails made with seasonal fruit.

Thai Chicken Lettuce Wrap includes grilled chicken breast, fresh vegetables, peanut sauce and lettuce cups. The Ryoshi Fresh Fish is an entrée salad piled high with fresh grilled fish, mixed lettuce greens, tropical fruit salsa, and vegetables. If you're into poke bowls, try the Nobu; a big, heaping bowl of fresh 'ahi poke, shelled edamame, cabbage, onions, sprouts, carrots, tempura shrimp, a crisped Spam steak, furikake white rice, teriyaki glaze, wasabi creme and tortilla strips for crunch. Burger aficionados may like the "Tamagotchi," with two onion rings, hard fried egg, mild kimchi, furikake, Korean kale sauce and lemon aioli.

"WE BELIEVE LOCAL SOURCING IS REALLY IMPORTANT, ESPECIALLY ON KAUA'I. BY SOURCING LOCALLY, WE KEEP MONEY IN OUR LOCAL ECONOMY AND PROVIDE A PRODUCT THAT IS FRESHER AND BETTER TASTING. GELATO IS ALL ABOUT SIMPLE INGREDIENTS, FRESH INGREDIENTS, PRESENTED BEAUTIFULLY. SO SOURCING LOCALLY ALLOWS US TO ENSURE WE ARE PROVIDING AN AUTHENTIC AND BEAUTIFUL PRODUCT."

MARCK SHIPLEY, OWNER AND GELATO ARTIST, PAPALANI GELATO

KAUAʻI BEER COMPANY

4265 Rice St., Līhuʻe
808-742-7207
www.KauaiBeer.com
Craft Brewery, California Cuisine

Jim Guerber and his son Justin opened Kauaʻi Beer Company in 2013. What began as a humble craft brewery, serving beer just two days a week, has bubbled into a lively hangout that's added food to its hoppy offerings.

"At KBC, it's all about the beer," says Chef Joe Fox, a former cook at Merriman's Fish House in Poʻipū and founder of the Kauaʻi Brew Club. "I make food that tastes great with beer but doesn't fill the diner up."

Līhuʻe Lager, the brewery's flagship beer, is light and crisp. At 4.8 percent Alcohol By Volume (ABV), the beer is on the light side of medium-bodied with a pale straw color, clean finish and faint hop aroma. At 3.8 percent ABV, Black Limousine is a light-bodied, dark lager with notes of chocolate and coffee. Seasonal beers have included Summer Saison, Austrian Chicken (Vienna lager), Tropical Armadillo (pale ale), Citra and Amarillo IPA and Zythos and Falconers Flight IPA.

Joe uses ingredients from local businesses such as Midnight Bear Breads (See page 157 for the full listing), Malamā Kauaʻi Community Farm, Kauaʻi Fresh Farms, Lāwaʻi Valley Mushrooms, Anahola Fresh, Kauaʻi Kunana Dairy and Kikala Farm. The Beer-brined Jerk Chicken Panini with scallion lime aioli is, hands-down, the most flavorful sandwich I've had on Kauaʻi. Juicy chicken thighs are crusted in a 13-ingredient, smoldering spice mix that Joe learned how to make while living in the Bahamas.

Menu listings have included Pork Belly Steam Bun slider with a soy and Līhuʻe Lager glaze; oxtail braised in Black Limousine with tomatoes, bell peppers and black beans served over rice; and house-made beef and pork bratwurst braised in beer and served with coconut green chili taro-potato mash, pickled red onions and citrus glazed greens.

*Kauaʻi Beer Company's pork belly sliders
on a steamed bao bun*

93

KAUA'I PASTA LĪHU'E

3-3142 Kūhiō Hwy., Līhu'e
808-245-2227
www.KauaiPasta.com
Italian

Kaua'i Pasta has two locations on the island, but their main one is located in Kapa'a. If you turn to page 60, you can read the complete description.

MISOYAKI

GORGEOUS IN ITS SIMPLICITY, SAKE-SOY GLAZED BUTTERFISH IS NOT A TYPE OF FISH, BUT A PREPARATION HERE IN HAWAI'I, ALSO KNOWN AS MISOYAKI. ANY FIRM-FLESHED FISH WILL WORK, AND THE COOKING PROCESS LEAVES A LIGHT CARAMELIZED COATING AND SWEET FLAVOR.

"SOURCING LOCALLY IS THE WAY MENUS ARE DEVELOPED IN MY ESTABLISHMENTS. BY TAKING WHAT IS CURRENTLY THE MOST DELICIOUS INGREDIENTS AVAILABLE AND PAIRING THEM WITH EACH OTHER, I FEEL LIKE WE EXPLORE WHAT HAWAI'I REGIONAL CUISINE REALLY IS. WE USE TRUCKLOADS OF MY HOME-GROWN PAPAYAS, BASIL, BANANAS, PUMPKINS AND CASAVA, PLUS LOCALLY GROWN COCONUTS, ORANGES AND NONI. BUT LET'S BE HONEST AND ADMIT THAT WITH A MILLION VISITORS PLUS THE GROWING RESIDENT POPULATION, IT WILL ALWAYS BE NECESSARY TO IMPORT MOST OF OUR FOOD. MY SMALL OPERATION USES TONS OF DAIRY, WHEAT, GRAIN AND TOMATO PRODUCTS THAT WILL ALWAYS BE SHIPPED. I SAY PRESERVE THE TERM 'LOCALLY SOURCED' BY NOT OVER-USING IT. BE HONEST AND SAY, '10 PERCENT LOCALLY SOURCED AND 90 PERCENT SHIPPED IN!'"

THOMAS PICKETT, OWNER AND BAKER, KĪLAUEA BAKERY

LĪHUʻE BARBECUE INN

2982 Kress St., Līhuʻe
808-245-2921
Japanese and Hawaiian

BLD$$ 👡 🌿

Līhuʻe Barbecue Inn is a humble diner that has been family owned and operated since 1940. Diners appreciate the old-fashioned aloha and well-rounded meals. Current owner Millie Sasaki has worked in the restaurant since she was a young woman married to the founder's son, Henry. Her daughter, Donna Muramoto, who now manages the business, grew up in the restaurant. The two ladies greet everyone who walks in, often asking about parents, children and grandchildren.

"We haven't changed our original concept of giving you a whole meal," Millie says. "It started out with homemade bread and butter, soup or small salad, then your entrée and your dessert. Our food has always been home-cooked, not commercial."

Fresh fish is served with gourmet sauces and the Macadamia Nut Crusted ʻAhi Salad with honey lime dressing is sweet and tangy. The Kālua Pork and Cabbage Plate, which is filled with smoky pork and tender cabbage, is a fantastic rendition of local comfort food. Japanese meals are served with pickled vegetables and a little somen salad instead of dessert.

Tender pork ribs with a house-made sauce

Each meal comes with dessert and you get to choose from about 15 varieties of cream pies made fresh daily. My favorite is the coconut cream pie with a coconut graham cracker crust. If you're too full, don't even think about taking it with you. Millie told me about a couple who were visiting and took their dessert to go. They drove around the island all day and got sick from eating it later that night. After that, Millie decided pies could only be consumed on the premises.

The prices are more than reasonable; parking is limited.

MAHIKŌ LOUNGE

Kilohana Plantation
3-2087 Kaumuali'i Hwy, Līhu'e
808-245-9593
Cocktails

Mahikō Lounge is located in the living room of the Wilcox family's former mansion at Kilohana Plantation. Jeanne Toulon, Director of Business and Public Relations for Kōloa Rum Company, swears this hidden secret employs some of Kaua'i's best bartenders. The word "mahikō" means sugar plantation in Hawaiian and many of the cocktails, including the Gaylord's Mai Tai, are made with fresh-pressed sugar cane juice.

Furniture imported by original owners, Gaylord and Ethel Wilcox, are reupholstered in rich, eclectic fabrics. A handcrafted, solid teak bar seats 16. Linen-fold wood molding, which matches the home's trim, as well as updated fixtures have been installed. Vintage black and white photographs depict renowned Hawaiian musicians, past celebrations and historic landmarks. A sound system connects the Mahikō Lounge piano to speakers throughout the mansion.

The Happy Hour menu is small and includes $5 items such as 'ahi poke, kale pork quesadilla and hot wings. A full dinner menu is offered at the adjacent Gaylord's restaurant. A Bloody Mary Bar opens every Sunday morning and live music at the piano bar and on the outdoor stage are part of the weekly lineup.

An enjoyable evening can be spent at Kilohana Plantation. First, swig rum samples at Kōloa Rum Company's Tasting Room (check koloarum.com for times). Then sip tropical cocktails made with Kōloa Rum at Mahikō Lounge, and end the evening with dinner at Gaylord's.

*Summer and Bonnie enjoying a Mai Tai made with Kōloa Rum
and fresh pressed cane juice at Mahikō Lounge*

MARK'S PLACE

Puhi Industrial Park
1610 Haleukana St., Līhu'e
808-245-2522
www.MarksPlaceKauai.com
American and Hawaiian

Mark's Place is a very popular takeout diner owned by Chef Mark Oyama and his wife, Wendy. Mark, an instructor for the Culinary Arts Program at Kaua'i Community College, also owns of Contemporary Flavors Catering.

"Mark has three philosophies," explains Wendy. "The most important is to provide good food, then good service and reasonable prices. Those three things together are what makes Mark's Place so popular."

Inside, a small counter fronts a large kitchen where a busy staff cooks meals to order, frosts wedding and birthday cakes, and fills catering orders. Pictures of loco moco and Korean chicken are taped to a glimmering stainless steel countertop and a sparkling cooler holds salads and desserts. A wire shelf labeled "Omiyage" holds packages of freshly made cookies, butter mochi and mini cake loaves. Omiyage (pronounced "o mee yah gay") is the Japanese tradition of giving gifts to co-workers, family and friends upon returning from a trip.

Local favorites include loco moco, chicken katsu and beef stew. There are also juicy hamburgers, French fries, Spam musubi and bento boxes. Pan Asian flavors and fresh ingredients are woven into daily specials, which are listed on a dry erase board and usually consist of two salads, three entrées and a dessert. Recent specials include cracked black pepper crusted shutome (Broadbill Swordfish) over kale salad with feta cheese and creamy Italian dressing; grilled chicken on a bed of vegetable pasta salad with baby greens; herb-crusted fresh opah drizzled with white balsamic vinaigrette; pork adobo with potatoes; chicken tofu stir fry and New York style liliko'i cheesecake with a pineapple compote.

Their Pau Hana Meal is a gourmet dinner that feeds a family of four and includes an entrée, side vegetable or salad, and dessert. Mark's Place posts daily specials on their website. The bustling diner is takeout only, with some picnic tables out front. We recommend calling in your order ahead of time.

Grilled Ahi with tomato salsa on a bed of noodles

NAUPAKA TERRACE

Aqua Kaua'i Beach Resort
4331 Kaua'i Beach Drive, Līhu'e
808-245-1955
www.kauaibeachresorthawaii.com
Hawai'i Regional Cuisine

When Rodman Machado became the executive chef in Dec. 2015, he created a new menu for Naupaka Terrace. Then in May, the resort began an $8 million renovation including new paint, carpet and lighting for each suite, as well as the lobby, banquet and restaurant.

Previously, Rodman was the chef de cuisine at O'ahu's Palm Terrace at Turtle Bay Resort. On Kaua'i, he was the executive chef at the former Garden Cafe, a farm-to-table restaurant where I had my first taste of lū'au, a luscious soup made with taro leaves and coconut milk.

Maui venison with breadfruit gnocchi

At Naupaka Terrace, Rodman makes lū'au with Tahitian taro from One Song Farm and drapes it over steamed rice which is topped misoyaki butterfish and lomi tomato relish. Polynesian Style Seafood Chowder includes fresh fish, mussels and scallops floating in a rich lū'au soup.

Healthy additions such as house-made hummus and vegetables brighten a lengthy and affordable breakfast menu. On the dinner menu, starters include an addicting organic kale salad with carrots, beets, jicama, macadamia nuts, avocado and a creamy miso vinaigrette as well as fire-roasted tomatoes topped with burrata cheese, balsamic vinegar, toasted garlic chips and fresh basil.

On Saturday nights, locals line up for the seafood buffet which features prime rib, an assortment of sushi and poke, crab legs, salads and an array of desserts. Watch for special farm-to-table dinners, which include beverages paired with Hawai'i made products. Previous dinners have included Maui Beer Co. and Kōloa Rum Co., where drinks such as Sage Advise (Kōloa Gold Rum with fresh sage, lemon and blueberries, Kaua'i honey, sea salt and a cracked black pepper rim) are paired with thyme roasted Moloka'i venison tenderloin.

The poolside bar serves shave ice for adults. Huge scoops of downy ice are topped with Kōloa Rum and mai tai or pina colada syrups, made by Hawaiian Blizzard Shave Ice Co. in Kapa'a.

Papalani Gelato

3366 Waʻapa Road, Līhuʻe
808-246-2060
www.PapalaniGelato.com
Frozen Dessert and Candy

Papalani Gelato has two locations on the island, but their main one is located in Poʻipū. If you turn to page 134, you can read the complete description.

Gelato flavors available for the whole family

PIETRO'S

3501 Rice St., Līhuʻe
808-245-2266
www.facebook.com/pietroskauai
Pizzaria

In Aug. 2016, Tommy and D'Lizza Iannucci opened Pietro's Pizza, which serves two types of pizza two ways: New York though a takeout window and Neapolitan inside an industrial-looking restaurant. Soon, the Iannuccis will own the only certified pizzeria in Hawaiʻi.

"It's a huge thing among pizza operators," says Tommy, who as of this printing, was waiting for accreditation from Associazione Vera Pizza Napoletana. "It doesn't mean much to the average Joe, but for anyone who knows that seal, they know they're eating as close to traditional Neapolitan pizza as possible."

As a child growing up in New York, Tommy was accustomed to great pizza. While he traveled the world as a Unites States Marine, he found global pizza depressing. Tommy was stationed at the American Embassy in Tokyo when he met D'Lissa, who was a model. The two married and in 1988, moved to Kauaʻi where she was born and raised.

When Tommy wasn't preaching at Breath of Life Church in Līhuʻe—which he still does every Sunday—he was making pizza at home. He lined the kitchen oven with clay tiles and made pizza for the guys at the fire department. He took pizza classes in New York and Italy, attended annual pizza expos in Las Vegas and finally, installed a brick oven in his driveway.

For Pietro's Pizza, he trained in Naples with Enzo Coccia, who Tommy says is one of the top five pizza guys in the world. The Iannuccis renovated the former Feral Pig restaurant and installed monkeypod wood pallets for a modern feel. Black and white photos of Tommy's family line the walls and pizza is made with Italian flour and tomatoes inside a brick-oven that was made by hand in Naples.

Diners can enjoy big slices of New York pizza, with beer or wine, on the outdoor patio. Inside, the Neapolitan pizza is thin and crackly and topped with gourmet ingredients such as white truffle paste and bresaola (cured beef). Wine is available by the glass or bottle, Italian beer is on tap, and five types of dessert liquor are available, including limoncello. Dessert includes Nutella calzones and Zeppole, fried dough balls topped with powdered sugar.

RAINBEAU JO'S

Halalu Street and Hoʻolako Street, Līhuʻe
808-652-5166
www.RainbeauJos.com
Espresso, Smoothies, Sandwiches

Rainbeau Jo's, a food truck parked on Hālau Street just south of Vidinha Stadium in Līhuʻe, serves breakfast, granitas, fruit smoothies and gourmet coffee drinks. Owners Beau Hannafious and Jordan Weaver also serve an outrageous side of aloha.

Jordan, who goes by "Jo," created their signature blend with beans from Hammerhead Coffee. The company, which is located in Bellingham, Washington, roasts and sells fair trade, organic beans that were sourced from small coffee farms around the world.

"Humidity effects how espresso shots pull. When we first moved here, my shots didn't have the crema I like," say Jo of the tawny colored liquid at the beginning of the extraction process. Ultimately, the light-colored liquid infuses with a dark liquid that comes after, leaving a tan colored layer on top of the darker espresso below. "I worked at getting my grind down, which I have to adjust about six times throughout the day, and now the crema is perfect, with a little black layer on the bottom and full creaminess on top."

Besides a "cup of Jo" and espressos, latte specials have included Gingerbread, Hula Girl with vanilla sugarcane, Honeycomb, Pumpkin Spice and White Peppermint Mocha.

Bullet Proof Coffee combines Velvet Elvis, a blend of smooth, dark roasted beans, with organic unsalted butter from grass-fed cows and organic coconut oil. Tim Ferris, author of "The 4-Hour Chef," created the recipe, which fits into the high-fat/low-carb Cross Fit Diet. (Kauaʻi Crossfit is located right next door).

"Cross fitters believe that if you start your morning with butter, it kick-starts your metabolism and the coconut oil helps you focus," Jo explains. "It gets me jacked up, and coffee doesn't do that to me!"

Granitas are a blend of espresso, ice cream, ice and Ghirardelli sauce. Blends have included Kauaʻi Cruiser with Ghirardelli chocolate; White Cap with Ghirardelli white chocolate; Caramel Haze with Ghirardelli caramel and hazelnut syrup and Funky Monkey with Ghirardelli chocolate; local apple bananas and peanut butter.

Breakfast is created with locally made organic bagels and has included Early Bird with pesto cream cheese, cracked pepper and local tomatoes, as well as The Honey Badger with organic butter and local honey compound.

Friendly service from Jo and Beau means your coffee is always served with a smile!

THE RIGHT SLICE

Harbor Mall
3501 Rice Street, Līhu‘e
808-212-8320
www.RightSlice.com
Pie Shop

The Right Slice has two locations on the island, but their main one is located in Kalāheo. If you turn to page 138, you can read the complete description.

A pie to go bananas for

ROB'S GOOD TIMES GRILL

4303 Rice St., Līhu'e
808-246-0311
www.KauaiSportsBarAndGrill.com
Sports Bar

It's dark inside Rob's Good Times Grill but neon lights and numerous television screens brighten things up. Rob Silverman and his wife, Lolly, have owned and operated this establishment since 1992.

"You gotta stay current," Rob says. "It's not the same thing you saw 10 years ago."

One of the things that's different is the menu. You can get the standard sports bar food you'd expect, such as burgers and hot sandwiches, but Rob's also offers sushi, entrées and a lengthy pūpū list.

All burgers are made with 8-ounces of locally raised grass-fed beef, fresh ground turkey, or buffalo. Favorites include a marinated and grilled portobello mushroom sandwich with greens, basil pesto, sautéed bell peppers, and Havarti cheese. Daily lunch specials have included lightly grilled 'ahi filet on wilted watercress with balsamic vinaigrette and home-style meatloaf. Brown rice and tossed greens are healthy options to replace Hawai'i's ubiquitous white rice and macaroni salad. There's a sushi bar on Sunday and Monday nights and a daily happy hour from 3 to 6 p.m. You'll find karaoke, DJ nights, live music, swing dancing, and, of course, sports. Rob tells me that by 9 p.m., it's often standing room only.

Every Sunday during NFL season, Rob's opens for breakfast and serves classics such as biscuits and gravy, or pancakes and bacon. Crepes, burritos, Hawaiian French toast and fried rice with eggs are also on the NFL menu.

SHAVE ICE

HAWAIIAN PIDGIN IS A LANGUAGE ALL ITS OWN AND IF YOU SPEAK TO SOMEONE WHO WAS BORN AND RAISED HERE, YOU MAY NOT UNDERSTAND THEM. MANY WORDS ARE SHORTENED, SUCH AS "SHAVE" IN "SHAVED ICE." SO IF YOU WANT TO SOUND LIKE A LOCAL, SAY "SHAVE ICE" INSTEAD OF "SHAVED ICE."

SKINNY MIKE'S HAWAIIAN ICE CREAM

Harbor Mall
3501 Rice Street, Līhu'e
808-245-9386
www.skinnymikesicecream.com
Ice Cream Shop

Skinny Mike's Hawaiian Ice Cream is a family-owned and operated business that serves ice cream and sorbets made with local fruit as well as sundaes, milkshakes and coffee produced in Hawai'i.

Waffle cones are made in-house so the smell of caramelized sugar fills the air-conditioned dining area. Twenty-four sorbets and creams fill the cooler. Sorbets include dragonfruit; mango sorbet; ube (purple sweet potato); lemongrass; lychee; and POG (pineapple, orange and guava). Ice creams include ginger; pineapple; and Kona coffee.

Dan's favorite is mocha java chip but I prefer the lychee cream. One bite, and the essence of sunshine fill my senses. The taste is floral and lightly sweet with bits of fruit, and it's as fresh as a summer breeze.

Wake Up Shakes are made with coffee instead of milk. There are also options for vegans and those on gluten-free diets. A cooler holds other beverages such as Kaua'i Juice Co. kombucha, Kona Red coffee berry juice, Wai Koko coconut water and Wailuā soda. A bench made from half a boat is next to the cooler, and wood tables and chairs are inside as well as outdoors on the lanai.

Sundaes include The Honu, with house-made caramel sauce, butter pecan ice cream, house-made hot fudge and whipped cream, and the S'more with macadamia nut ice cream, graham crackers, house-made hot fudge and roasted marshmallows.

Mocha Java Chip in a waffle cone

TIP TOP CAFE

3173 Akahi St., Līhu'e
808-245-2333
American and Hawaiian

Līhu'e Plantation built the Tip Top Building in 1916 and its main tenant was a cafe and bakery named after the structure. Denjiro Ota was a cook for the plantation manager who asked him to open a coffee shop so people could have breakfast and coffee in the mornings. In 1925, Denjiro's son, Mitchell, took over the business and created macadamia nut cookies and banana pancakes, which are still popular today. Plantation era food still dominates the menu at the business which is now officially known as the Tip Top Motel Cafe & Bakery.

The outside looks dated but don't let that stop you. Rows of padded bench seats inside the spacious building are filled with people immersed in animated talk and laughter. It's not fancy or five-star, but the clean diner is a local hang-out where kind, waitresses in brown dresses serve traditional favorites. Hearty portions of loco moco, saimin, beef stew and fried rice are served from rolling dimsum carts. Their popular oxtail soup consists of tender meat that clings to beef tailbones in a pale, flavorful broth. Lightly cooked Chinese cabbage is added to the soup, which is served with a side of steamed rice as well as grated ginger and minced cilantro. If you didn't come with a large appetite, however, try the half order.

Breakfast favorites include pancakes topped with macadamia nuts, pineapple or bananas, cooked on one side, and then flipped. Standard menu items include bacon, ready-made hash browns, fried eggs and omelets.

Longtime locals know this place gets packed and they hold confidential business meetings because the boisterous dining crowd makes it impossible to eavesdrop.

SEASONS ON KAUA'I

WHEN VISITORS ASK IF THERE ARE SEASONS ON KAUA'I, I SAY, "YES! MANGO SEASON, BANANA SEASON, LYCHEE SEASON AND AVOCADO SEASON." OF COURSE I'M ONLY JOKING, BUT WE DO HAVE SEASONS. SUMMER IS BLAZING HOT AND DRY AND THE BEST TIME FOR TROPICAL FRUIT. THE TRADE WINDS STOP BLOWING THROUGH KAUA'I AROUND AUGUST AND RETURN SOMETIME IN OCTOBER. IF YOU LOOK HARD, YOU'LL NOTICE THE VEGETATION IS A LITTLE BROWN. THINGS COOL DOWN IN THE FALL WHEN THE RAINS BEGIN AND BY WINTER, IT CAN RAIN EVERY DAY. DURING THE FALL AND WINTER MONTHS, VEGETATION IS LUSH AND VERDANT AND THE WHALES HAVE MIGRATED FROM ALASKA TO HAVE THEIR BABIES. IN THE SPRING, THE DAYS BEGIN TO GET WARM AND DRY AGAIN.

TORO TEI

Kaua'i Marriott Resort
3610 Rice St., Līhu'e
808-245-5050
Sushi

Toro Tei Sushi Bar is tucked along the lavish courtyard of Kaua'i Marriott Resort, attached to Kukui's restaurant. With views of Kalapaki Bay and a menu of affordable sushi, it's a lovely way to enjoy an evening with friends and family.

'Ahi is No. 1 grade A, sourced locally and fresh—"no frozen blocks gassed with CO_2," says Executive Chef Guy Higa. Hamachi comes from Japan, farm-raised salmon comes from New Zealand and Kaua'i Shrimp is grown on the West Side. Real king and blue crab are also on the menu.

Imagine dipping your sushi in melted butter. It sounds weird, but it's brilliant. The Baked Crab Nigiri features two plump strips of king crab and broiled blue crab mixed with wasabi mayonnaise. Dipping the decadent bite into lemon butter adds a sublime richness that is extremely satisfying.

The first time I spoke with Chef Higa, I was new to sushi. I'm from Colorado, where buffalo and trout reign supreme, so he explained some common sushi terms to me.

"Anytime you see nigiri on a menu, it means two. Like this," he said, pointing to the Kaua'i Quail Egg and Tobiko Nigiri. "Anytime you see temaki, that means cone," he said, nodding towards two emerald cylinders loaded with lobster, wasabi mayonnaise and avocado.

"This is a real traditional dish," he said of the Chirahsi Bowl. "It's a chirashi, which means scattered sushi, but we Americanized it." Instead of fish piled into a bowl, Chef Higa has created a symmetrical arrangement of crab, shrimp, salmon, tako (octopus), hamachi and 'ahi on a row of sushi rice.

"Maki sushi means a roll," explained Higa, while pointing to Da Spida with deep-fried blue crab legs emerging from its center.

The Bento Roll is Chef Higa's idea of a bento box in a roll. "It's got barbecued beef, some daikon, shrimp tempura, furikake rice and tamago," he said. "It's everything that you would find in a bento."

"Tamago is an art to make," he said of the flakey omelet. "A lot of people buy it frozen, but it's all spongy. It's horrible. We make ours and it's nice and light and moist."

Lobster and crab temaki at Toro Tei

107

SOUTH SHORE

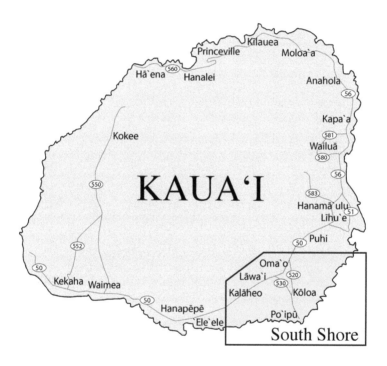

Heading into Kōloa Town, you drive down Maluhia Road, also known as the Tree Tunnel

ANUENUE CAFE

Po'ipū Shopping Village
2360 Kiahuna Plantation Drive, Poipu
www.AnuenueCafe.com
American

Anuenue Cafe is a family-owned breakfast spot that opened in the Po'ipū Shopping Village in Sept. 2015. Michelle Hastings manages the restaurant while her husband, John Adams, is the chef, and their daughter, Kendall, is a server and photographer. You can see Kendall's work lining the walls as you order at the take-out counter. After placing your order, pick a spot outside at one of the covered picnic tables where Kendall will bring your meal.

"When I was a private chef on O'ahu, we had a lot of killer fish markets," says John, who has been a chef for 28 years. "I got used to using local, fresh ingredients and made things like liliko'i -chardonnay butter-sauce served over opah."

At the cafe, you'll find items such as the Haupia Mac Nut French Toast, made with thick chunks of cinnamon-spiked Hawaiian sweetbread--a chilled cube of house-made haupia sits on top under a pad of melting butter. It's delightful as it is, but the crushed toffee-colored macadamia nuts make it a terrific treat.

Eggs Benedict are served two ways and come with herb roasted potatoes. The Duck Dive (don't be fooled by the names!) is vegetarian and includes spinach, tomato and two fried eggs. The Riptide has piles of salty kālua pork. Both are

Wife and husband team, Michelle Hastings and John Adams

Keanu Reeves Eggs Benedict: one veggie and one with kalua pork; seasonal fruit plate and a cup of Pakala blend coffee

draped in a thick Meyer lemon hollandaise sauce. If you can't decide, ask for Keanu Reeves, and you'll get one of each.

"We have a Meyer lemon tree in our yard," explains John. "I clarify my own butter and make the hollandaise fresh every morning. For the kālua, we sprinkle pork shoulder with Hawaiian sea salt, wrap it in banana leaves and cook it for 22 hours."

Risotto Moco is an upscale twist on the local favorite, Loco Moco. John chars a patty made from Makaweli Meat Company's grass-fed ground beef. It's mixed it into the risotto with a flavorful gravy. Caramelized Lāwa'i Valley oyster mushrooms are placed on two fried eggs and the whole thing is drenched in more gravy.

The Belly Flop is Michelle's recipe. She makes giant, super-moist coconut macaroons that are studded with lime zest and served with a generous scoop of Papalani Gelato's vanilla bean gelato.

"We like to share what this island has to offer and support small family businesses," says Michelle. "Plus, we've found that when people come here, they want to taste Kauai."

John flexes his creative muscles during monthly four-course tasting dinners, which are held at the cafe and have included Niihau Ranch grilled lamb chops with a baked potato and local thyme torte, watercress and tzaziki sauce. And that's just one course! Check their Facebook page for event details.

Nora, Paula's sister, along with four other chefs cook authentic Thai food at Bangkok Happy Bowl.

BANGKOK HAPPY BOWL

Po'ipū Shopping Village
2360 Kiahuna Plantation Drive
808-742-9888
http://m.mainstreethub.com/bangkokhappybow
Thai and Japanese

Kirk Coult and his wife Paula Rungsawang-Coult own Bangkok Happy Bowl. Paula is from Thailand and her family recipes fill the lengthy menu. Her sister Nora, along with four other chefs from Thailand, cooks curries and noodle dishes in the restaurant's kitchen.

"We didn't have a refrigerator when I was young," recalls Paula, "and it was long before grocery stores, so we had to buy fresh ingredients every day."

"That is a typical market in Thailand," says Kirk, pointing to a large painting on the wall near the restaurant's front door. "You buy produce and fish from people in boats on the river."

Paula's menu is infused with produce grown by a Thai farmer on the South Shore and all curries, pastes, broths and hot sauces are made from scratch. Flavorful chili sauces range from garlicky, to pleasantly warm, to fiery. Paula says many Thai restaurants use vinegar for the sour element, but she insists on using authentic tamarind sauce.

Here's a tip for those who do not like food laced with chili peppers: scan the menu for dishes without a chili pepper logo by its name. These have no heat. Those with one chili pepper have a pleasantly mild heat, but if you like it hot, look for two chili peppers. Tell the waitress you'd like it "Thai hot" if you want to burn your face off!

Pla Lad Prig is a house specialty that features a deep-fried whole fresh snapper that's coated in an aromatic sauce of kaffir lime, tamarind pulp and fish sauce. It's topped with sautéed bell peppers, fried basil leaves, garlic, lemongrass and chunks of ginger.

If you don't like heat, order the Massaman Curry with potatoes, carrots and toasted peanuts. I like the mild heat in the Green Curry. Eggplant, grown by the local Thai farmer, floats in a complex sauce with strips of chicken, crisp broccoli, carrots, Thai basil, green beans, red bell peppers, celery and zucchini. Po'ipū Rock'n Roll Sushi is a separate restaurant inside Bangkok Happy Bowl, with an extensive menu that includes shrimp dumplings, tempura calamari, poke salad, sushi rolls and green tea ice cream.

Satay Chicken comes with with peanute sauce and cucumber sauce

H HOUSE RESTAURANT

22 Lāwa'i Rd., Kōloa
808-742-1424
www.The-Beach-House.com
Hawai'i Regional Cuisine

Nestled along Po'ipū Beach, The Beach House restaurant offers ocean views and spectacular sunsets. Dinner includes fresh fish and seafood with rich sauces and fresh salsa, but there's plenty for meat lovers, too. One of the most popular dishes is the Wasabi Crusted Fresh Island Catch. Pungent wasabi and flaky panko coat pan-fried fish, which sits on a bed of Big Island green beans and julienned carrots sautéed in white wine and butter. A garlicky pilaf of long-grain rice and Bhutanese red rice accompanies the dish. A silky liliko'i lemongrass butter sauce flecked with black sesame seeds surrounds the whole thing.

Lunch includes affordable options such as the Stir-Fried Vegetable Bowl with a scoop of white rice and a mix of fresh vegetables tossed in a tangy soy-ginger sauce. The Kālua Pork Sandwich comes with a side of fries and is served on a bun that's made fresh every morning. Topped with a slaw of fresh pineapple, papaya, rice wine vinegar and mayonnaise, it's a sweet and tangy addition to the smoky-salty house-made pork.

Dubbed "One of the Most Romantic Restaurants in Hawai'i" by *The Travel Network*, The Beach House has won 26 awards including *Wine Spectator* magazine's Award of Excellence for 2009 and 2010.

Handcrafted Restaurants, which is headed by renowned Hawai'i chef Peter Merriman and restaurateur Bill Terry, purchased the Beach House Restaurant in May 2016. Although Handcrafted Restaurants owns the popular Monkeypod Kitchen chain, Terry says there are no plans to covert it into a Monkeypod.

Cocktails and an ocean-side view at the Beach House

CHALUPAS

3477 Weliweli Road, Kōloa
808-634-4016
www.ChalupasKauai.com
Mexican

Growing up in Veracruz, Mexico, owner Miguel Baldera was always in the kitchen helping his mother and abuela (grandmother) prepare meals. Today, Chalupas is his baby. The food truck serves grab-and-go Mexican food using family recipes and carefully chosen ingredients. Miguel serves up tasty food in a flash, and the menu allows you to mix and match your heat and meat. Besides the barbacoa (beef braised with herbs and spices) and carnitas (pork braised with herbs and spices), you can choose from marinated and grilled fresh fish, chicken or steak.

Local pork from Kaneshiro Farms is slow cooked in a zesty Veracruz tomatillo sauce, resulting in succulent carnitas; Kalāheo beef is braised for hours, rendering a tender and juicy barbacoa. A local baker makes fresh bread for The Torta, an enormous Mexican sandwich traditionally filled with carnitas. A variety of salsas are made fresh daily as well as the cabbage slaw, which is made with cucumber, carrots, onions, cilantro, lime juice and olive oil.

The Chalupa is like a tostada only the tortilla isn't dry and crunchy. Two semi-fried corn tortillas are smothered with beans, meat, cabbage slaw, tomato, fresh avocado, salsa, pickled jalapenos and queso fresco. With beans and rice on the side, it makes a delicious, budget-friendly meal.

HAWAIIAN SUPERFOOD

NONI IS ONE OF THE "CANOE CROPS" THAT WERE BROUGHT TO THE ISLANDS BY THE ORIGINAL POLYNESIAN SETTLERS. STUDIES SHOW THAT NONI IS 75 PERCENT AS EFFECTIVE AS MORPHINE AT KILLING PAIN, AND THAT'S JUST ONE OF A LONG LIST OF BENEFITS. THE FRUIT IS NOT POPULAR, MOST LIKELY BECAUSE IT TASTES AND SMELLS LIKE BLUE CHEESE. THAT'S OKAY WITH VEGANS BECAUSE THEY USE NONI TO MAKE "BLUE CHEESE" SALAD DRESSING! IF YOU'D LIKE TO LEARN MORE ABOUT THE HEALING PROPERTIES OF NONI, OR TRY SOME OUT, CHECK OUT HAWAIIAN ORGANIC NONI FARM IN MOLOA'A. FOR MORE INFORMATION, VISIT WWW.REAL-NONI.COM.

DA CRACK

2827 Po'ipū Road, Kōloa
808-742-9505
www.DaCrack.com
Mexican

Da Crack is literally a crack in the wall but once you try it, you'll be hooked. Tucked between Kukui'ula Market and Outfitters Kaua'i, Da Crack is just a 10-foot-long take-out counter. Fresh, never frozen, grass-fed beef and natural chicken are braised for hours and lovingly coaxed into savory and healthy Mexican dishes. Fresh fish caught in Kaua'i's waters is seasonal and cut to order.

Cubes of pork shoulder, also fresh and natural, are browned and braised for five hours with Da Crack's seasoning blend, fresh tomatillos, tomatoes, onions and guajillo, chipotle and jalapeño chilies. The same cooking technique is used for the chicken and beef, and the result is succulent animal protein.

"I do everything to the extreme," explains owner Danny Hurtado, a former semipro surfer and mixed martial artist. "I'm kind of a perfectionist, in a way, and if I don't like something, then why would I think that someone is going to come to my window and like it?"

Mix and match protein, rice, beans, salsas (mild, medium or hot) and guacamole to create your own giant burrito, taco, or have it naked, in just a bowl. Brown rice is the only option, and you can order it plain or with Mexican flavors. Salsas and guacamole are made fresh daily, and flaky flour tortillas (no corn here) are cooked to order. Tender black beans and pinto beans are cooked without animal products. I always order the brown rice bowl topped with kālua pork, guacamole and hot salsa.

Da Crack serves up The Ono Bowl with extra guacamole. Delicious and nutritious.

THE DOLPHIN

The Shops at Kukuiʻula
2829 Ala Kalanikaumaka St., Kōloa
808-742-1414
www.HanaleiDolphin.com
Fresh Fish and Sushi

The Dolphin has two locations on the island, but their main one is located in Hanalei.

If you turn to page 21, you can read the complete description.

ʻAhi Teriyaki served with steamed rice and grilled vegetables

> *"I AM ABLE TO USE ALL THE FRESH AND LOCAL INGREDIENTS THAT ARE AVAILABLE TO US ON KAUAʻI. MY APPRECIATION FOR QUALITY INGREDIENTS HAS COME FROM MANAGING ORGANIC FARMS ON KAUAʻI'S NORTH SHORE FOR THE PAST 11 YEARS."*

SETH PETERSON, OWNER AND CHEF, KICKSHAWS

NDERO'S

Grand Hyatt Kaua'i Resort & Spa
1571 Po'ipū Road, Po'ipū
808-240-6456
www.Kauai.Hyatt.com/en/hotel/dining/Donderos.html
Italian

Dondero's delivers great service, terrific food and spectacular ocean views. Guests dine al fresco on the scalloped portico, which is flanked by flaming tiki torches. Their black silhouettes are stark against the setting sun, as orange flames dance against the blue sky and lavender-tinged clouds cling to the ocean. As the sun sets, palm trees press against an indigo sky and stars begin to make an appearance.

Our favorites include Peppered Beef Carpaccio, which is made with beef tenderloin encrusted with cracked black pepper, seared and thinly sliced. It's meltingly tender and sweet from a balsamic vinegar and currant reduction. Briny black olives, dry ricotta cheese and dehydrated capers add a tangy contrast. Underneath, there's a pasta basket with fresh greens and pickled shallots.

Osso Buco is a hefty portion of tender meat, house-made pasta and a robust pan sauce made with onions, carrots and celery. Once the vegetables are sautéed, the pan is deglazed with demi-glace, red wine, veal stock and tomatoes. Veal shanks are added and braised for up to five hours in a pressurized oven. The dish is garnished with a gremolata of minced parsley, garlic, lemon and orange zest. The shank is loaded with creamy marrow, which you can spoon onto toasted ciabatta bread.

Broth for the Cioppino is made with tomatoes, tomato paste, marinara sauce, onions, bell peppers, lobster and fish stock. The broth curls around house-made pasta, poached Tristen lobster tail, fried obsiblue (New Caledonia shrimp), grilled fresh fish and grilled scallops. When available, clams or crab also make it into the dish.

After dinner, we typically walk around the lush property and meander down winding walkways that cross over river-like swimming pools and koi ponds that intertwine throughout the property. Couples swim in the pools, which reflect starlight from a bottomless sky. Hula girls wearing coconut cups teach men how to shake their hips during the oceanside lū'au on Sunday and Thursday evenings. Along the beachfront, rows of whitecaps crash into the bay and a cool breeze rides the still night. As we make our way back to our room, we sit on a wood bench and watch the moon's reflection shimmer on the water.

Osso Buco and bone marrow

EATING HOUSE 1849

The Shops At Kukui'ula
2829 Ala Kalanikaumaka Road, #A-201, Kōloa
808-742-5000
www.EatingHouse1849.com
Hawaii Regional Cuisine

When Roy's closed its doors at the Po'ipū Shopping Village in March 2015, the staff headed over to The Shops at Kukui'ula and opened Eating House 1849. While designing the concept, Roy Yamaguchi took inspiration from Peter Fernandez, a Portuguese businessman who opened one of Hawai'i's first restaurants. Eating House also evokes Yamaguchi's grandfather, who owned a tavern and restaurant in Wailuku, Maui during the 1940s.

When Roy envisioned the restaurant, he pictured family-style dining, where people order big platters of food to share, similar to the plantation era. The open-air dining room has wood floors and high ceilings with large beams and the kitchen is surrounded by glass, which enables an unobstructed view of the ocean. You can watch chefs create food that borrows flavors and techniques from Hawai'i's immigrant cultures: Japan, China, Spain, Portugal, Korea, Puerto Rico, and the Philippines.

Dishes are rustic and comforting compared to a typical Roy's fine-dining menu. The Corn Beef Reuben, for example, is layered with house-made brisket, Gruyere cheese, caramelized onions, shredded cabbage and "1849" Thousand Island dressing, served on a taro bun. Wild boar raised on Hawai'i Island is ground with Makaweli Meat Co. beef for the Hapa Burger. Huli Huli Style Spicy Pork Belly starts with

The broth of this saimin is not to be missed!

a brine then the belly is cooked sous vide (vaccum-sealed and slow cooked), to preserve flavor, moisture and texture. The belly is sliced, drenched in a Korean-style marinade with spicy go chu jang made with rice vinegar, sugar and shoyu. The slices are diced into bite-sized pieces and grilled to order, so they're charred and crispy. It's served with romaine lettuce, kimchi, Korean vinaigrette, pickled scallions and crispy garlic.

My favorite dish is the 1849 Spicy Ramen Bowl where pork bones are used to make a rich sesame broth. The massive bowl comes with two shrimp and pork dumplings, soy-braised pork belly, a roasted Roma tomato, spiced and sautéed ground pork and a soft-boiled egg.

KALĀHEO CAFÉ & COFFEE COMPANY

2-2560 Kaumuali'i Hwy., Kalāheo
808-332-5858
www.Kalaheo.com
American and Hawaiian

Open since 1994, the Kalāheo Café & Coffee Company specializes in roasting and selling fine coffees produced on Kaua'i and in the state. Owners Kris and John Ferguson are committed to providing high-quality coffee backed by ethics.

"No Kona blends," says John, referring to the dishonest practice of adding 10 percent Kona coffee to inferior beans and calling it Kona coffee. "We only sell 100 percent extra fancy and peaberry, which are the two finest grades available."

Inside, fans whirl from a high ceiling and sparkling glass counters are filled with freshly made apple pie, carrot cake and their popular coconut custard cake. The decor's warm colors, such as burnt sienna and milk chocolate, mirror house-baked goods and specialty coffee drinks.

For breakfast, you can order from a long list of espresso and coffee drinks, hot meals or fresh pastries. Lunch includes deli sandwiches, salads, burgers and wraps. Dinner features upscale and healthy options such as the Quinoa and Spring Veggie Bowl, Grilled Fresh Catch and Baked House-Made Turkey Meatloaf. Weekly specials include the local favorite, Slow-Roasted Prime Rib of Beef.

Kalāheo Cafe mahi mahi with pesto aioli

KALAPAKI JOE'S

1941 Poʻipū Road, Poʻipū Beach
www.KalapakiJoes.com
808-742-6366
American and Hawaiian

Kalapaki Joe's has two locations on the island, but their main one is located in Līhuʻe. If you turn to page 92, you can read the complete description.

Kalapaki Joe's serves a variety of dishes using fresh island fish

HAWAIʻI'S FOOD SECURITY

"ABOUT 85 TO 90 PERCENT OF HAWAIʻI'S FOOD IS IMPORTED, WHICH MAKES IT PARTICULARLY VULNERABLE TO NATURAL DISASTERS AND GLOBAL EVENTS THAT MIGHT DISRUPT SHIPPING AND THE FOOD SUPPLY," STATES A 2012 REPORT BY THE HAWAIʻI DEPARTMENT OF AGRICULTURE CALLED "INCREASED FOOD SECURITY AND FOOD SELF-SUFFICIENCY STRATEGY."

THIS, COMBINED WITH MORE THAN 1 MILLION VISITORS ANNUALLY, MAKES IT EXTREMELY DIFFICULT FOR RESTAURANTS TO SOURCE 100 PERCENT OF THEIR PRODUCTS FROM THE STATE, LET ALONE KAUAʻI. THAT IS WHY WE FEEL IT IS IMPORTANT TO SUPPORT ESTABLISHMENTS THAT MAKE THE EXTRA EFFORT TO SOURCE LOCALLY AS MUCH AS POSSIBLE.

KAUA'I JUICE CO.

Po'ipū Shopping Village
2360 Kiahuna Plantation Drive, Kōloa
808-634-0886
www.KauaiJuiceCo.com
Cold-Pressed Juice Bar

The Kaua'i Juice Co. has three locations on the island, but their main one is located in Kapa'a. If you turn to page 59, you can read the complete description.

SHRIMP & CLAMS

SOME LOCAL RESTAURANTS SERVE KAUA'I SHRIMP AND KAUA'I CLAMS, WHICH WERE RAISED IN SALT WATER PONDS IN KEKAHA. BOTH ARE SWEET AND PLUMP. THE SHRIMP ARE SOLD FRESH, WITH THEIR HEADS AND TAILS STILL ON. MANY RESTAURANTS LEAVE THEM INTACT TO SHOW THEY ARE KAUA'I SHRIMP. LOCAL GROCERY STORES, SUCH AS FOODLAND AND ISHIHARA MARKET, SELL THE FRESH SHRIMP, WHICH YOU CAN COOK IN YOUR HOME OR VACATION RENTAL.

Lush landscaping makes a perfect tropical atmosphere at Keoki's Paradise

KEOKI'S PARADISE

Po'ipū Shopping Village
2360 Kiahuna Plantation Drive, Kōloa
808-742-7534
www.KeokisParadise.com
Hawaii Regional Cuisine

"Keoki's Paradise captures that feeling you get when you walk into your friend's back yard. It's the lifestyle, aloha and sharing food that we grew up with," says Executive Chef Cory Dotario. "If Keoki was an uncle, it's like you're coming into his house to have a pa'ina (party)."

Inside seating is on a lanai that overlooks a pond, which trickles into a stream, then into another small pond and down a little waterfall. Tropical flowers as well as palm and bamboo trees rustle in the trade winds and a giant banyan tree throws deep shadows. Laughter from outside diners mixes with Hawaiian music and spills across the restaurant, where rustic beams stretch its length and lazy fans hang from vaulted ceilings.

The menu includes grass-fed beef and each day about five varieties of fresh fish hang in the kitchen's cooler. The Chef's Fresh Fish Duo, in fact, allows you to select two 3-ounce portions of the daily catch (misoyaki seared or herb grilled) with citrus vinaigrette, Thai coconut jasmine rice, and vegetables. Seasonal fresh fish is also used in a succulent Ginger Cilantro Steamed Fish, which is topped with Asian pesto (made with cilantro, ginger, sesame oil and scallions), sizzling peanut oil and citrus ponzu sauce. Grilled Thai Shrimp on a Green Papaya Salad includes local mixed greens, carrots, tomatoes, green beans and peanuts in fresh lime vinaigrette.

From 4:45 to 5:45 p.m., the Chef's Sunset Menu includes a starter, entrée and dessert for $24. There's live music every night and Aloha Hour is every day in the Bamboo Bar from 3 to 5 p.m. Half-price appetizers (pūpū) and specials on select entrées are available as well as tropical drinks, wine by the glass and draft beer. Specials include Kālua Pork Cheese Fries with pickled red onions, cilantro and roasted tomato aioli; sliders with local, grass-fed beef; and fish tacos.

Save room for their popular Hula Pie, a gargantuan slice of macadamia nut or mint chocolate chip ice cream on an Oreo crust drizzled with hot fudge and topped with whipped cream. Every month, Keoki's showcases a hula pie flavor-of-the-month, which has included chocolate with salted caramel and "haupia" with toasted coconut flakes.

KICKSHAWS

3540 Kōloa Road, Kalāheo
808-651-6750
www.Kickshaws.webs.com
Gourmet Sandwiches

Seth Peterson likes to play with his food. With a Bachelor of Science in biology, a job at Kailani Farms in Kīlauea and a food-loving heart, his dive into molecular gastronomy seems natural. Also known as "science forward food," the discipline attracts inquisitive chefs who take traditional tastes and textures, and flip them on their head.

When we spoke, he wore a blue T-shirt with the molecular structure for umami, a name for savory, which is one of five basic tastes. Under the diagram was printed: "OOH-Mami. I want more."

His light-hearted approach tempers over-the-top molecular gastronomy. Seth's use of scientific techniques for his sandwich-based menu is simple. For his 100% Awesome Burger, salt, chuck short-rib, sirloin and bacon are put through a meat grinder. As the mixture is extruded, it's kept horizontal. When it's cut, the strands are short, making the burger extremely tender. He tops it with pineapple, black pepper and onion marmalade, Gouda cheese, mayonnaise, arugula and tomato.

Pork belly is typically used to make bacon, but in the PBAT (pork belly, arugula and tomato), it's cooked for six hours, sous vide. This technique involves cooking food in vacuum-sealed pouches that are submerged in water and held at a precise temperature. Once the pork belly is exceptionally tender, Seth crisps it on the grill and tops it with arugula, tomato, pickled mustard seeds and apple wood smoked mayonnaise.

Seth created the spicy Tempeh Banh Mi for his vegan friends. His spin on the Vietnamese sandwich includes tempeh (fermented soybeans) marinated in yellow curry, then seared on the grill. Topped with coconut Sriracha mayonnaise, smoked soy sauce gel, pickled carrots, cilantro oil and cucumber, it's the most flavorful vegan sandwich I've ever had.

The PBAT: Pork belly, arugula and tomato

You can also find their truck at Hanapēpē Art Night as well as Warehouse 3540 in Lāwa'i. Occasionally, Seth cooks a multi-course tasting menu in a fine dining setting. When we went, the menu was internationally inspired and included nine courses for $75. The price covers the meal, tax and tip, but you have to bring your own beverage. Check their Facebook page for special events.

KŌLOA DELI

5476 Kōloa Road, Kōloa
808-742-9998
www.Facebook.com/Koloa.Deli
Subs and Italian

BL $ 👡 🍃

Owner Ron Magrin grew up on an artichoke farm in California, which also raised cows, pigs and chicken for meat and eggs, and had a family garden. Ron's grandparents emigrated from Northern Italy, and he learned how to cook by watching his grandmother make large amounts of food for the ranch hands. He says his grandmother never went to the store; she cooked whatever was produced on their farm.

Ron brought his grandmother's recipes and ethos to Kaua'i and opened Kōloa Deli where everything is made from scratch. Lasagna and spaghetti are layered with house-made and locally sourced meat sauce. Soups include Portuguese Bean (offered monthly) and a buttery Clam Chowder with big chunks of tender clams.

Subs are made with bread that is baked in-house every morning. The Godfather, a zesty specialty sandwich, is loaded with Genoa salami, capocollo, mortadella, prosciutto, provolone, onions, lettuce, artichoke hearts, pepperoncini, olive oil, vinegar and fresh oregano.

Daily specials include hot sandwiches such as the Hot Chick--served on a toasted roll with buffalo chicken, pepper jack cheese, pepperoncini, onions, tomato, lettuce, mayo and ranch dressing--and the BBQ Pulled Pork sandwich with slow-cooked pork shoulder that's tossed in a house-made BBQ sauce and topped with coleslaw.

Ron has an 8-acre ranch in Lāwa'i where he raises grass-fed beef. He uses it in sandwiches or specials, and sells select cuts from the deli cooler. The deli also serves breakfast sandwiches, deli salads and soup. We think these guys have the best subs on the island and the best garlicky Italian Bean Salad we've ever had.

Peppermill chicken, avocado and bacon sandwich

125

KŌLOA FISH MARKET

5482 Kōloa Road, Kōloa
808-742-6199
www.facebook.com/Koloa-Fish-Market-Inc
Hawaiian

On Sept. 11, 1992, Hurricane Iniki struck Kauaʻi with such force, many local businesses never recovered. Three Poʻipū hotels were severely damaged by the storm, including the Sheraton Kauaʻi Resort, where Bert Matsuoka had been the executive chef for 24 years.

"I didn't know what to do," recalled Matsuoka, who graduated from the Culinary Arts Program at Kapiʻolani Community College in 1961. "I wanted to do a lunch wagon for a long time, something to do with plate lunch. I had a friend in Honolulu and I saw all the fresh fish, so I thought I would do something with that.

Matsuoka opened the Kōloa Fish Market in 1994 in Old Kōloa Town. Today, he only accepts cash and he feeds hundreds of customers a day. The tiny space holds a cooler with house-smoked marlin, dried aku, scallop salad and seven varieties of poke. Fresh ono, ʻahi, mahimahi, blue marlin, opah and monchong are sold by the pound. In the back, a six-burner gas stove poaches chicken for long rice. On another burner, a pot of laulau steams. Pork ribs, which are cooling in a tidy prep kitchen just behind the stove, will be added to house-made barbecue sauce for the daily special.

"We run three specials a day," says Matsuoka. "Today, we have seared ʻahi with caper butter, teriyaki or wasabi cream sauce. I like a little bit of each sauce. There's also beef curry stew and chicken cutlet with gravy. Yesterday we had Korean chicken, seared ʻahi and meatloaf."

Jason, Bert and Randy Matsuoka

There are always three Hawaiian plates to choose from: laulau, kālua pork or a combo. Each comes with two scoops of rice, mac salad, lomilomi salmon, chicken long rice and a small cup of poke.

LA SPEZIA

5492 Kōloa Road, Kōloa
808-742-8824
www.LaSpeziaKauai.com
Italian

After running Casablanca in Poʻipū for 10 years, owners Elizabeth Foley and Dan Seltzer closed their resort restaurant in 2013 to open La Spezia in Old Kōloa Town. In 1997, the couple opened Dali Deli on the east end of the Old Town Shops, and this is where the family-run business returned.

Light jazz plays on the sound system and crystal chandeliers dangle from chocolate-colored ceilings. Black-and-white family photographs hang on beige walls, including one taken in the family's apartment in Rome on Via Spezia, which means Spice Road. Tables that Foley handcrafted from wine crates are topped with small vases of fresh herbs. A temperature-controlled wine cellar holds 100 varieties ranging from $18 to $120.

Mia Foley, Elizabeth's daughter, blends cocktails behind a monkeypod and limestone bar. As a former bartender at Seattle's Tavern Law and Rumba, Mia learned to use fresh juice in her balanced and refreshing cocktails. Cocktails change regularly and have included, Tequila Mockingbird, made with lemon and pineapple juice, Sauza Blue Silver tequila and St. Germaine elderflower liqueur. Ciao Bella, made with Maui's organic Ocean Vodka, limoncello, lemon juice, and basil, is topped with a Fragoli Wild Strawberry float, which contains tiny, handpicked wild strawberries.

The small menu is loaded with Italian classics. Meals start with fresh ciabatta bread, topped with chunky sea salt and a blend of poppy and celery seeds, and served with extra virgin olive oil and balsamic vinegar.

One item you don't find on many Italian restaurant menus is hanger steak, which is packed with flavor. At La Spezia, it's cooked medium rare, sliced thin and piled on pan-seared polenta infused with Gorgonzola cheese. Sautéed green beans, a rich house-made demi glace and briny olive tapenade make a bold dish that holds its own, especially when paired with a robust Sangiovese produced by Farnese, a 16th Century Italian vineyard.

No need to make reservations, La Spezia prefers a casual, walk-in approach. If you are on an alternative diet, just let them know when you order.

Hanger Steak with Farnese Sangiovese

LIVING FOODS MARKET & CAFE

The Shops at Kukui'ula
2829 Ala Kalanikaumaka St., Kōloa
808-742-2323
www.ShopLivingFoods.com
California Cuisine

Living Foods Gourmet Market & Cafe is owned and operated by Jeff Sacchini (founder of The Kaua'i Marathon) and his brother-in-law, Howard Warner. It's easy to get lost in the air-conditioned store, perusing aisles for gourmet pantry items. Hawai'i-grown coffee is roasted onsite and more than 300 bottles of wine and 20 types of beer are offered. Local produce and imported cheese are stacked alongside house-made sauces and condiments, such as olives marinated in roasted garlic, orange zest, chili flakes and fennel seeds.

Banderillas, a sweet, spicy and earthy red sauce, works well on seared steak or grilled 'ahi. Salsa Verde, with chunks of egg whites, capers, cornichons, onion, herbs and garlic, is delicious on sausage or fried eggs with toast. Spicy romesco sauce with a sherry vinegar tang, is fabulous on potatoes or roasted meat. Aioli, a lemon-garlic mayonnaise, is great over just about anything including steamed vegetables, paella, seared white fish, seafood or grilled lamb chops.

At the butcher counter, Kaua'i Shrimp and Kaua'i Clams are stacked next to trays piled with glistening fresh Hawaiian fish, Duroc Farms free range pork, chicken breasts and house-made sausages including chicken, Italian, and Portuguese.

In the cafe, specialties include banh mi (a Vietnamese sandwich) with house-made Asian pork meatballs, pickled vegetables and cilantro with Sriracha mayo on French bread. "Have it your way" Poke Bowls include toppings such as pineapple and macadamia nuts and deli sandwiches are made to order. Pizza is also made to order and cooked in a Wood Stone oven. Breakfast includes lemon ricotta pancakes with blueberries and maple butter, and gluten-free crepes filled with fontina, smoked ham and a soft egg. The juice bar makes drinks, smoothies and açaí bowls to order including the Hawaiian Glow with coconut water, pineapple, cucumber, spinach, kale and ginger. A large menu of prepared salads includes Crunchy Miso with cabbage, almonds, cilantro, sesame oil and rice wine vinegar, as well as a Farro Salad with shallots, garlic, capers, parsley, olive oil, tomatoes and fresh mozzarella.

MAKAI SUSHI

Inside Kukui'ula Market
2827 Po'ipū Rd., Kōloa
808-639-7219
Sushi

Makai Sushi is inside Kukui'ula Market, a family-owned grocery store located in Kōloa. Walking in, Matthew Oliver's sushi bar is just to your left. The slender young man, dressed in a black Japanese chef's jacket, works behind a thick coconut bar that he made. Matthew's ready smile and local-style teasing defies the serious sushi chef.

"Saddle up guys!" Matthew calls to a middle-aged man and his pre-adolescent son. "Don't be shy. I don't bite!"

They order the 'Ahi Poke Bowl, which is like deconstructed sushi in a bowl. Sushi rice is pressed into the bottom, and then topped with a small handful of ocean salad (seaweed), and fresh daikon (radish) spirals. Spicy 'ahi poke is placed on top and the whole thing gets a drizzle of wasabi ailoi, unagi sauce and spicy yogurt sauce. Tobiko, green onions, sesame seeds and furikake are sprinkled on top. As you eat, the flavors and textures meld with the creamy sauces, making the dish delightfully more interesting as you eat.

Sitting on wood stools at the high bar, a young couple from Seattle, Washington orders the Hapa Roll. Matthew quickly places a full sheet of nori on a sushi mat and presses rice up to the corners. A broad wood bowl contains 35 cups of steamed rice, which Matthew mixed with fermented vinegar. He tops the rice with spicy 'ahi, blue crab, thinly sliced white onions, avocado and cucumber and tucks the bottom over the top, swiftly using the sushi mat to produce a large, tight roll and cuts it into fat rounds. Matt drizzles the Hapa Roll with unagi sauce and a spicy sauce made with no fat Greek yogurt. There's a final flourish of sesame seeds and furikake, then a gentle placement of tobiko (fish eggs), a nob of wasabi paste and a tangle of pickled ginger.

Matthew Oliver serving up some mega-sized rolls

129

N'S FISH HOUSE

at Kukui'ula
alanikaumaka St., Kōloa
85

www.MerrimansHawaii.com
Hawai'i Regional Cuisine

In the early 1980s, Peter Merriman was at the forefront of putting the organization, Hawai'i Regional Cuisine, on the map. He made the calls and invited a group of chefs to the first meeting. As president, he introduced chefs to Hawai'i Island farmers, encouraging them to use as many fresh, local ingredients as possible.

"Peter has great relationships with farmers," says Mark Arriola, executive chef of Merriman's Po'ipū. "We really push ourselves to make sure at least 80 to 85 percent of everything we serve is from the Hawaiian Islands."

The upscale restaurant is located on the second floor of The Shops at Kukui'ula. Open walls offer a glimpse of the ocean, and ceiling fans spin reflections on gleaming wood floors. Framed black-and-white photographs of Kaua'i's farmers, posed like rock stars, line the walls.

"We're really big about building relationships with our farmers and fishermen," says Arriola, as Cynthia Chiang of Kaua'i Kunana Dairy jogs up the stairs with today's delivery. "Hi chef!" She calls out, and slips through the back door and into the kitchen.

Preferring the superior quality in flavor and texture, Merriman's sources from local fishermen who troll the shores of Kaua'i, and deliver their fresh catch hooked earlier in the day.

"We like troll caught, because the quality of the fish is better," Arriola explains. "With long line fishing, the fish go through more stress, they sit in the water for a long time, they sit on the boat even longer. We want day boat fish."

Macadamia Nut Crusted Mahi Mahi, caught by Lee Zeidner on the West Side, includes a sake mushroom reduction, local green beans and roasted eggplant. Merriman's Original Wok Charred 'Ahi, caught by Captain Cody Kimura, includes won bok (Napa cabbage) slaw and wasabi soy sauce. Olive Oil Seared Ono, caught near Ni'ihau by Nathan Berg, includes Umi Farms kale, lemon, local squash, fresh tomato and garlic sauce.

"As a chef, I love that I know who grew my stuff," Mark says. "There's a face to everything that comes in our door. That adds more responsibility, and you take more care. When I'm preparing dishes with their food, I know they support their family with it. For me that's the coolest thing."

Happy hour includes discounted poke as well as mai tais with passion fruit foam.

MERRIMAN'S GOURMET PIZZA & BURGER

The Shops at Kukui'ula
2829 Ala Kalanikaumaka St., Kōloa
808-742-8385
www.merrimanshawaii.com/gourmet-pizza-burgers
American

Merriman's Gourmet Pizza & Burgers is below Merriman's Fish House. The casual eatery showcases local produce, meat and fish, for which Merriman's is known.

The Vegan pizza is made with house-made organic wheat crust and topped with roasted Hamakua mushrooms, Hirabara Farms Kale, macadamia nut "Parmesan" and tomato sauce. Roasted Hamakua Mushroom pizza is served with white sauce, roasted Hamakua mushrooms, truffle oil, tarragon, thyme and parsley. Sweet Shrimp & Toasted Garlic is topped with white sauce, sautéed sweet shrimp and toasted garlic. All pizzas are available on gluten-free crust for an additional charge.

Fresh Island Fish and Kālua Pig Carnitas tacos are topped with fire roasted tomato salsa, local cabbage, avocado-lime crema and cilantro in a corn tortilla.

Meat eaters can choose between a free-range, natural turkey burger with caramelized onions, aged white Cheddar, Asian pear and organic arugula; Teriyaki Burger with grass-fed beef from Makaweli Meat Co., Kaua'i Roots Farm watercress, vine-ripened tomato, mayonnaise and house-made teriyaki sauce; or, for the gluttonous meat lover, the B.K.E. (Beef, Kālua, Egg) Burger. This behemoth is served on a pillow-soft bun made with Kaua'i Beer Company's Black Limousine, a dark lager that's also available on tap. Tucked inside, a Makaweli Meat Co. patty is topped with house-roasted kālua pork, slow-cooked onions, house-made kimchi and a fried local farm egg.

Happy hour includes discounted poke as well as mai tais with passion fruit foam.

Merriman's lobster pizza is simply amazing

D JAM

ali'i Hwy., Lawa'i
8
podjam.com

BL $$ 🩴 🍃

Aletha Thomas is in her commercial kitchen cutting slices of cara cara oranges. She covers them in water and leaves them to sit in a pot overnight. In three days, it will become a thick marmalade mixed with fresh ginger. Boxes filled with 200 pounds of Kaua'i Sunrise papayas wait to be made into fruit butter with cinnamon and nutmeg, or papaya and vanilla bean jam. Aletha walks to a gas stove and stirs 25 pounds of Meyer lemons in a copper pot. Bubbles slowly burst in the thick syrup and she turns off the heat.

Aletha's Liliko'i Curd (passion fruit) is ranked number 45 in *Saveur* magazine's 2016 Top 100--an annual survey of the world's best gourmet food products. In 2009, Aletha was a schoolteacher with extra time due to Furlough Fridays (a program that closed Hawai'i's public schools for 17 Fridays). She'd make jam with local and seasonal fruit and sell it in pint-sized jars with handwritten labels at the farmers markets. In Nov. 2015, she opened a cafe and store in Lāwa'i. The shop currently produces about 55 types of jams, curds and marmalades, and Aletha works with about 40 local farmers.

In the front, behind the counter, quart-size jars of Moroccan lemons sit on a wood shelf, gleaming in a sunbeam. A fisherman stops by to pick up ice, which Aletha sells by the pound. Kirra Yoshioka hands customers tiny spoons with samples of thick jam, which can be spread on a locally made bagel and eaten it at a small wooden table.

Chef Jodi Agena makes sandwiches with local eggs or roast chicken; a daily soup; quiche layered with Aletha's spiced tomato jam; house-made yogurt; cream cheese and mango jam danishes; puff pastry filled with scrambled eggs, vegetables, bacon and cheese; and frozen treats called whips.

"Whips are frozen local fruit and have included white pineapple, mango and banana," says Aletha.

Since school busses stop in front of the shop, any keiki (child) wearing their school shirt receives $1 off from 2 to 4 p.m.

Follow Monkeypod Jam on Facebook for upcoming workshops, which have included pickling, growing succulents, making marmalade, preserves and haku lei. Most workshops are four hours and include spritzers and dinner made by chef Jodi.

After you eat, bring home jam made from local fruit

PACO'S TACOS CANTINA

At Kukuiolono Golf Course
854 Pu'u Road, Kalāheo
808-332-5792
www.pacostacoskauai.com
Mexican

Tony and Paco Aguilar are from the Mexican coastal area of Ixtapa-Zihuatanejo. The brothers brought their experience of working in five-star hotels to Kaua'i and opened Paco's Tacos, a local franchise with three outlets including Paco's Tacos Lighthouse in Kīlauea and Paco's Taco's House in Kapa'a. Paco's Tacos Cantina, which opened in 2015, is the only location that also serves cocktails.

Paco's son, Francisco works behind the bar. Dime-sized silver grommets pierce both of his ears and he wears a shirt that says, "'I hate tacos,' said no Juan ever." A Paco's Tacos logo covers the back of his tee and his soft smile and easy voice make you feel like you're in good hands.

There are 20 types of tequila behind the bar. Purists will appreciate the Top Shelf Margarita, made with fresh lime juice, triple sec, and a Hawaiian sea salt and li hing mui rim (see glossary). House margaritas include tequila, triple sec and a sweet and sour mix.

Wide windows reveal views of the ocean, a golf course, palm trees and mountains. Big screen TVs hang in corners and play sports at a low volume. While their wives enjoyed spa time at the Grand Hyatt Kaua'i, a father and his two sons rented golf clubs and played nine holes of golf for a total of $70, then finished their day with lunch here.

A large menu, which is the same at the Kapa'a location, includes breakfast, tortas (Mexican sandwiches), tacos, burritos and salads. Specials have included menudo and house-made chorizo. "Paco's Favorites" lists the house specialties such as the Carne Asada Fries, which are like nachos but with French fries, topped with melted cheese, top sirloin, guacamole, sour cream and pico de gallo.

Tortillas are cooked to order and burritos are served plain, enchilada-style with red sauce and sour cream, smothered with pork chili verde, or chimichanga style (fried), and served with guacamole, lettuce, sour cream and pico de gallo. The Al Pastor burrito is loaded with juicy pork, pineapple, crisp lettuce, rice and beans. It's filling and a great deal if you're really hungry.

The South Shore location even enables the brothers to offer regular entertainment such as live music, as well as wine and painting workshops.

Paco Aguilar and his son Francisco

133

PAPALANI GELATO

Po'ipū Shopping Village
2360 Kiahuna Plantation Road, Po'ipū
808-742-2663
www.PapalaniGelato.com
Frozen Dessert and Candy

At Papalani Gelato, Marck and Lauren Shipley make and sell premium gelato, sorbetto and chocolates. Everything is handmade, including the marshmallows, caramel, toffee, macadamia nut butter and peanut butter cups that go into the gelato and chocolates. Papalani means "heavenly" in Hawaiian, and gelato means "frozen" in Italian. On any given day, there are 33 flavors to choose from.

The main difference between ice cream and gelato is air content. When you add an ice cream base to a commercial machine, it gets whipped and incorporates 50 percent air.

"When we put a gallon in, we get just over a gallon out," explains Marck, referring to their gelato machine. "It's a much healthier product. Ice cream has so much air in it they have to put in added fat because when air freezes it turns to ice. So the more air you have, the more fat you have to add to keep ice crystals from forming."

Salt Pond gelato is made with Hawaiian sea salt, and was inspired by a gift the Shipleys once received of salt harvested from Hanapēpē. *Honolulu* magazine called Papalani Gelato's chocolate gelato one of the best in the state. The sorbettos are rich, creamy, thick and decadent, and flavors such as lychee, lemon, pineapple, blood orange and mango make frequent appearances. Local favorites include pineapple-li hing mui; haupia (which is made in-house and folded into the gelato base); chocolate-ginger; and kūlolo, a Hawaiian confection made with taro and coconut milk.

Papalani Gelato at Anchor Cove in Līhu'e serves a smaller gelato menu. A full coffee bar uses Hawaiian and organic beans and there are also all natural frozen drinks, locally made pastries and a selection of Kaua'i Made products.

Serving up 33 flavors of gelato and sorbetto

PIZZETTA

5408 Kōloa Road, Kōloa
808-742-8881
www.PizzettaRestaurant.com
Italian

Old Kōloa Town's charm extends into Pizzetta's Italian-themed restaurant. Diners can sit on the lanai where banana trees, an herb garden, taro plants and colorful flowers rustle in the trade winds and vintage Hawaiian music plays softly on the sound system.

BBQ Baby Back Pork Ribs, which were featured in Bon Appétit magazine, include a generous portion of slow-cooked pork in a homemade papaya barbecue sauce with a spicy kick. Pastas include Fettuccine Quattro Formaggio and Brown Rice Penne Cecca with basil, tomatoes, garlic and spinach. Chicken Milanese includes Parmesan-crusted chicken breasts atop garlic mashed potatoes, julienne-cut zucchini and carrots, and a delectable white gravy.

Make-your-own pizzas and calzones include toppings such as meatballs, anchovies and kālua pork, plus 16 types of vegetables, as well as pineapple. Specialty pizzas include kālua pork and cheese and shrimp puttanesca. A thin and chewy crust is the base of Pizza Paradiso, which is loaded with pesto, grilled chicken, fire-roasted vegetables and topped with feta cheese. Warning: when you sink your teeth into the pie, your mouth is treated to a creamy and savory bite, which may cause a deep exhale of relaxed comfort.

The Fettuccine Lucia will have you dining with a smile at Pizzetta

PLANTATION GARDENS RESTAURANT AND BAR

2253 Po'ipū Road, Kōloa
808-742-2121
www.PGRestaurant.com
Hawai'i Regional Cuisine

Plantation Gardens makes you feel like you're escaping to Old Hawai'i. In the parking lot, a giant monkeypod tree stretches 50 feet into the air, its branches creating a cocoon of sorts. Along the walkway, there is a trickling stream, lava koi pond and more than more than 1,200 orchids.

The restaurant is tucked inside the Moir Estate, originally owned by Kōloa Sugar Plantation Manager Hector Moir and his wife, Alexandra "Sandie" Knudsen. The manor, made of lava bricks, was a wedding gift from Sandie's father in 1930. The Pau A Laka Garden (meaning, "skirt of Laka," the Hawaiian goddess of hula) is located west of the restaurant, where there is also an 80-year-old cactus.

Plantation Gardens specializes in fresh fish and light flavors, and the cocktail menu features refreshing drinks made with fruit and herbs. Seafood Laulau, with a combination of fresh local fish, large prawns, jumbo scallops and julienned vegetables are steamed and presented in a ti leaf. Local fish is crusted with smoked quinoa and served with creamed quinoa, asparagus and tomato chili oil. Pot roast is served with kabocha (squash) mash, oyster mushrooms, edamame, madeira glazed onions, sesame-lemon crumbs and red wine demi-glace.

Handcrafted cocktails include the Sunburst Margarita with cilantro, lemongrass Sauza tequila, ruby red grapefruit, pomegranate, agave and freshly squeezed lime juice.

Every March, Plantation Gardens hosts a Royal Dinner during the two-week-long Prince Kūhiō Celebration, which celebrates the last reining prince of the Kingdom of Hawai'i before it was overthrown. The multi-course meal is made of traditional Hawaiian foods prepared in gourmet fashion.

HOW DOES THAT TASTE?

HAWAI'I REGIONAL CUISINE MEALS ARE THE FRESH, FLAVORFUL AND BEAUTIFUL DISHES YOU USUALLY SEE AT FINE DINING ESTABLISHMENTS. EXAMPLES INCLUDE AKU (SKIPJACK TUNA) POKĒ CEVICHE WITH ORANGES, TOMATILLOS AND AVOCADO; WATERMELON AND FENNEL SALAD WITH KAUA'I KUNANA DAIRY GOAT CHEESE; BRAISED WAILUĀ LAMB SHANK WITH SAFFRON RISOTTO; AND PAN-SEARED UKU (SNAPPER) WITH OKINAWAN SWEET POTATOES AND OKINAWAN SPINACH.

RED SALT

Koa Kea Resort
2251 Po'ipū Road, Kōloa
808-828-8888
www.KoaKea.com/Dining-At-Red-Salt
Hawai'i Regional Cuisine

In the lounge at Red Salt, diners enjoy pre-dinner cocktails while sitting on a round couch reminiscent of the 1960s, or white leather sofas with chocolate wood frames. The open dining room, with creamy travertine floors, high ceilings, and sweeping windows that offer ocean views, create a clean and elegant atmosphere.

On the menu, Red Salt's signature poke features a checkerboard of 'ahi and walu (Hawaiian butterfish). The glistening cubes sit on a bed of crisp wakame (seaweed) and sweet cucumber. There are dabs of spicy sauce on the walu, and tobiko (flying fish roe) adds a fun pop.

Vanilla Bean Seared Mahi is basted with butter and served with floral black rice that was soaked in fresh coconut milk. A knob of zesty avocado-ginger salsa and a swirl of tangy curry sauce add a flavorful contrast.

The Seared Rack of Lamb pairs four juicy Colorado-raised loin chops with blocks of mango gelée and mango chutney. A side of creamy cauliflower couscous puts fat beads of tender couscous against toothsome bits of lightly cooked cauliflower, which are tossed with garlic, shallots, butter and Pecorino cheese. A pool of tamarind glaze is flavored with house-made veal stock, wine, star anise, black peppercorns, lemongrass and coriander.

Breakfast entrées include local avocado on sourdough toast, lime and coriander; Butter-poached Kona lobster Benedict with local tomato, local avocado and mango hollandaise sauce; and Lemon-Pineapple Soufflé Pancakes with crème fraîche.

Red Salt Poke is a checkerboard of 'ahi and walu

137

THE RIGHT SLICE

2-2459 Kaumuali'i Hwy., Kalāheo
808-212-5798
www.RightSlice.com
Pie Shop

The Right Slice offers so many options, it's hard to pick just one. Owner and baker Sandy Poehnelt creates more than 45 varieties of sweet and savory pies. For those with dietary restrictions, she even offers options such as a gluten-free crust and no sugar added.

Her buttery piecrusts are rolled by hand and loaded with savory fillings. Mainstays include chicken potpie and Shepherd's pie. Vegetarian specials have included mushroom medley, or asparagus, black pepper and Parmesan cheese.

You can call ahead and have a hot potpie waiting for you, or you can take frozen ones home to bake. When we know we'll be in the area for lunch, we'll call ahead and order potpies.

Sweet fillings are numerous. Our favorites, made with Kaua'i-grown fruit, include Island Lime, Mango Liliko'i , Mountain Apple and Liliko'i Curd. An amazing 4 pounds of apple bananas goes into the Tropical Banana Pie. There is no custard to be found, just loads of firm bananas, cinnamon and a little pineapple juice. If you want something wicked, try the Chocolate Peanut Butter Banana Pie, laced with organic peanut butter and dark chocolate pudding.

Sizes include by the slice, deep dish (serves 8-10), baby (serves 4-6), Lotus Blossom (handheld pies), Menehune Bites (one bite), and Shaka Pops (lollypop pies).

Mango pie is a hit at The Right Slice

138

RumFire Po'ipū Beach

Sheraton Kaua'i Resort
2440 Ho'onani Road, Kōloa
808-742-4RUM (4786)
www.RumFireKauai.com
Hawai'i Regional Cuisine

Guests dining at Sheraton Kaua'i Resort's signature restaurant will enjoy 180-degree oceanfront views from all of its 240 seats. RumFire boasts two 10-seat communal tables fronting an open kitchen with a brick oven and Table 53 (more on this below).

Menu selections include a filet mignon on a bed of braised kale, juicy mushrooms and roasted garlic béarnaise sauce. Fingerling potato halves, caramelized from butter and heat, are nestled against the beef, along with house-made truffle cheese. The flavors are complex, layered and full.

RumFire's Hawaiian Paella is loaded with chunks of freshly caught fish and Kaua'i shrimp and clams, scallops and Portuguese sausage. The tender rice is cooked in a flavorful tomato sauce spiked with Portuguese sausage, corn and chayote squash.

There are 60 types of rum on the menu; 45 are boutique rums, including those from Kaua'i's own Kōloa Rum Co. RumFire's cocktail menu includes a kiawe (mesquite) smoked "Rum-Hattan (see back cover).

Desserts change frequently and have included chocolate fudge cookies, apple banana lumpia (Filipino egg rolls) with rum honey, and cinnamon apple cobbler--all are extremely comforting. One bite of the warm, double fudge chocolate cookie, for example, with Lappert's vanilla ice cream, and suddenly it's after school and I'm sitting at my mother's kitchen table. The brownie-like cookies have a crisp exterior and walnuts add crunch to the rich, moist interior.

All net proceeds from Table 53 are donated to Kaua'i's charities. Since its inception in 2012, more than $140,000 has supported Kaua'i's veterans, children and animals in need. A new charity is selected each month and donations have been awarded to non-profits including Kaua'i Philippine Cultural Center, Mālama Pono Health Services, Kaua'i Humane Society,

Quite possibly the best pork chop ever made, topped with bacon and a spicy sauce

..c Girls Club of Hawai'i, Kaua'i United Way and many more. Make sure to əst Table 53 when making reservations.

With rhythmic drumming and ukulele strumming, swaying hips and an imu pit, the Sheraton's Auli'i Lū'au includes Hawaiian-rooted cuisine, authentic costumes, and award-winning dancers. It's held on the resort's beach lawn and if you're lucky, a full moon will complete the picturesque setting.

A smoked Rum-Hattan really hits the spot

THE SOUP LADY

Kaua'i Culinary Market
2829 Ala Kalanikaumaka St., Kōloa
808-335-5011
Soup

Since 2003, Helen Lacono and her daughter, Andrea Pisciotta Kaohi, owned and operated the Hanapēpē Café and Bakery, which was known for its soups and salads. After an emergency trip to Wilcox Memorial Hospital due to a heart attack, Helen declined open heart surgery and 12 prescription medications, closed the café and decided to heal holistically. Today, she's bursting with youthful energy and serving the ultimate comfort food.

Every Wednesday afternoon at The Shops at Kukui'ula, Helen sells freshly made soup during the Kaua'i Culinary Market. As the market opens, people cluster around her table. Some come every week and know they always have four types of soups to choose from—all handcrafted in harmony with the seasons. Others are here for the first time and eagerly try samples.

"Most of my soups are very healthy," Helen explains. "In the program I was in, they encourage you to eat something warm first thing in the morning."

To heal, Helen used Functional Medicine, which addresses underlying causes of disease through a patient-centered approach. Practitioners learn patient history through lengthy examinations of genetic, environmental and lifestyle factors, which influence long-term health and chronic disease.

"My chicken soup is very healing for the body, and I make the broth from scratch," Helen says. "I try really hard to not use gluten and I use as much organic produce from this farmers market as I can. I like to support our farmers, they're wonderful people."

Each container holds 16-ounces of soup, or two cups. Helen's popular Hungarian Mushroom Soup is made with cream, butter, Hungarian paprika, loads of dill and button mushrooms. It's rich and creamy with a touch of cayenne pepper that gives it a little kick.

Helen's cookbook *Kaua'i Farmers' Market Soups* is available at the market and Talk Story Bookstore in Hanapēpē. In October 2013, she reopened Hanapēpē Café and Bakery (see page 152 for the full listing).

Helen Lacono, The Soup Lady, makes her soups from the heart and serves them with aloha

uth Shore

ᴐN'S LIBRARY

att Kaua'i Resort & Spa
pū Road, Kōloa
ᵢ456

www.Kauai.Hyatt.com/en/hotel/dining/StevensonsLibrary.html

Sushi

At Stevenson's Library, masculine elegance seeps from warm wood walls, floors and fixtures, inspiring an elegant and accommodating feeling. Patrons imbibe in an extensive selection of whiskies, cognac, port, sake, wine, martinis and tropical drinks at the opulent wood bar, or enjoy them on the lanai that overlooks the ocean.

Super-premium ingredients fill the sushi bar including Yamamotoyama nori wraps; $120-a-pound fresh wasabi (horseradish), which is available upon request, and fresh fish flown in six days a week from Japan's Tsukiji Fish Market and the Honolulu Fish Auction. There's also a ponzu sauce (citrus-soy)--a sauce so highly touted, it's served to the emperor of Japan--that takes six months to prepare.

The refrigerated sushi display case contains steelhead salmon raised in boutique aquaculture farms on the Faroe Islands. Rows of wild Japanese Hokkaido scallops sit plump and dry, promising firm, tender and creamy bites. Filets of hamachi, 'ahi and snapper are placed next to aji, a rich Spanish mackerel.

New items are added to the menu every three to four months. Recent maki (rolls) additions include Black Rock, an umami explosion with shrimp tempura and chili pepper 'ahi. Salmon is tucked inside the Kōloa, a sweet, crisp and creamy combination of mango and avocado with kampachi draped over the top. Cubes of 'ahi are rolled inside Shipwreck, which is draped with salmon and topped with crunchy garlic chips and thin rounds of jalapeño slices.

Sashimi presentations include moriawase, a large platter with freshly grated horseradish and thin slices of big eye tuna. Delicate sprays of purple seaweed, rosemary, pansy flowers, shiso leaves and daikon spirals are tucked around raw slices of snapper, salmon, hamachi and Big Island kampachi.

Additional favorites include Sushi Pizza served on naan bread and Lobster Tail Dynamite--a spicy blend of scallops, crab, shiitake mushrooms, white onion, tobiko and eel sauce stuffed into a lobster tail.

Lobster tail stuffed with dynamite sauce, scallop, crab, shiitake mushroom, white onion, tobiko and eel sauce

TIDEPOOLS

Grand Hyatt Kaua'i Resort & Spa
1571 Po'ipū Road, Kōloa
808-240-6456
www.Kauai.Hyatt.com/en/hotel/dining/Tidepools.html
Hawai'i Regional Cuisine

More than five million OpenTable.com reviews placed Tidepools, at the Grand Hyatt Kaua'i in Po'ipū, on the "100 Most Romantic Restaurants in America" list. It's easy to see why. The thatched-roof restaurant is in the middle of several large pools, which reflect sprays of fuchsia bougainvillea. A waterfall and swaying palm trees are amid the lush surroundings. Sitting in wicker chairs on a raised platform, you feel like you're floating in a gentle tide pool. Koi fish swim lazily in clear water that curls with the kiss of easy trade winds. When you add the fact that the South Shore is one of the best places on Kaua'i to catch a spectacular sunset, you've got an exceptionally romantic restaurant.

The Poke Duo is a fresh take on the ubiquitous poke tower. Cubes of tender 'ahi are placed on a round jasmine rice that's seasoned with a soy-mirin sauce. A tempura onion ring is placed on the 'ahi, which is topped with garlicky cubes of hamachi and flurry of slivered Maui onions, micro greens and tobiko sit on top. The perfect bite is a delightful combination of tastes and textures.

A Tidepools classic is the fresh opah with jumbo-lump crabmeat, roasted fingerling potatoes, snow peas, shiitake mushrooms, papaya-habanero sauce and balsamic drizzle.

*www.OpenTable.com users named Tidepools one of the top 100
most romantic restaurants in America*

The New York Steak is flavorful, juicy and tender. It's served with sautéed onions and Lāwa'i Valley oyster mushrooms, roasted fingerling potatoes, steamed broccolini and a silky Longboard Lager reduction.

The Tidepools creme brûlée is garnished with poached pineapple, crystallized ginger and toasted coconut. Again, a delightful combination of tastes and textures.

Watching the sunset over the ocean and the koi throw ripples in the water, it's hard not to drink in Kaua'i's beauty. Tidepools reflects that timeless Hawaiian allure and there's no question why it's voted one of America's most romantic restaurants.

Scorched Pina with roasted peppers, pineapple, lime, Hornitos tequila and dry Curaçao is just one of the amazing cocktails at Tortilla Republic

Tortilla Republic

The Shops at Kukui'ula
2829 Ala Kalanikaumaka St., Kōloa
808-742-8884
www.TortillaRepublic.com
Modern Mexican

The two-story building faces the courtyard of The Shops at Kukui'ula, and with no outside walls, diners can people watch while being fanned by the trade winds. Downstairs, in the Margarita Bar & Cantina, handcrafted cocktails are available such as the Hydration margarita made with coconut water. Order the tableside guacamole, custom made to suit your heat tolerance, and served with freshly made corn chips.

Lunch and dinner include quesadillas, tacos and burritos. The Machaca burrito involves a special Mexican technique, which includes dehydrating the beef and then rehydrating it in a saucy reduction of vegetables and juice.

"We sear a beef shoulder, and then braise it in garlic, onions and peppers for three hours," says co-owner Jordan James. "It's cooled, dehydrated for up to 12 hours and torn into large shreds. Dehydrating intensifies the flavors of the meat. It's a classic preparation in Mexico."

Upstairs, 10-foot-high Mexican wood doors carved with floral designs guard the entrance. A buttery onyx bar, also imported from Mexico, is lit from underneath. Contemporary world music plays, leather tables and pigskin chairs abound, and the servers wear dresses made by a local tailor. For a sumptuous Mexican dinner or Sunday brunch, reserve a table upstairs.

There are 80 tequilas behind the bar, and a full menu of margaritas, including the spicy Po'ipū Heat made with chili water and the Perfect Margarita made with lime juice, agave syrup and rimmed with flakey salt from England's Maldon Sea.

Tortillas and chips are made fresh everyday using masa harina, a corn flour made from freshly prepared hominy (dried maize soaked in an alkaline solution). Salsas are also made in-house and include salsa de mesa, a spicy blend of charred vegetables; the Oaxaca, made with dried pasilla peppers, sweet papayas and smokey chipotles; and the tomatillo salsa, which is garlicky, bright and slightly spicy. Los Tres Salsas is a bottomless tasting of all three, served with chips.

Entrées include roasted poblano pepper stuffed with eggplant, mushroom, spinach, toasted pine nuts, raisins, Serrano ham and cilantro citrus sauce, queso fresco and sour cream. The Short Rib Chile Verde is a spicy dish made with braised short ribs and roasted garlic jalapeño potato purée, topped with roasted tomatillo and jalapeño sauce and crispy red onions.

WEST SIDE

Sunset at Salt Ponds Beach Park in Hanapēpē

BOBBIE'S ISLAND RESTAURANT & CATERING

3824 Hanapēpē Rd., Hanapēpē
808-335-5152
Hawaiian

Bobbie's Island Restaurant & Catering is known for oversized servings of house-made meals. Owners Derek and Dawn Hosaka are siblings who were born and raised on the Westside and share an affinity for food and family. In fact, Bobbie's is named after their mother Barbara Hosaka, who passed away in 2001.

"My mother was an extraordinary woman," recalls Dawn, "and I wanted to name the restaurant after her to keep her memory alive."

Dawn's father was a commercial fisherman and as a child, she watched him make food for his crew. One Saturday morning he made scrambled eggs in the family kitchen. Dawn asked if he would teach her how, and in the process, she fell in love with cooking.

Derek took the culinary program at Washington State University, cooked in the college's kitchen, then came back to Kaua'i and became a chef at Wilcox Memorial Hospital.

Derek and Dawn created the recipes at Bobbie's, which include house-made tartar sauce, hand-shaped hamburgers and pork laulau. Sista's Fried Chicken are cubes of boneless chicken thighs sprinkled with a flavorful house-made spice blend, and that's it. It's served with garlic Parmesan dip, two scoops of rice and mac, or a fresh salad. Order a large fried saimin and you'll get a massive serving with bacon, eggs and fish cake.

"Large servings were my mother's philosophy," says Derek. "When she invited you to our home for a meal, she didn't want you to go home hungry."

Korean Chicken is a fiery blend of cubed, boneless chicken thighs that are drenched in flour and deep-fried. Straight from the fryer, they get a bath in Korean sauce made with garlic, chili peppers, brown sugar, soy sauce, sesame seeds and onion powder, and garnished with green onions.

Roast Pork is made with pork shoulder that's been braised for three hours. It's either shredded and served as a sandwich with house-made barbecue sauce or served with a rich and silky house-made gravy.

"It's all about love," Dawn tells me after I let her know it's the best brown gravy I've had on Kaua'i.

Every Friday during Hanapēpē Art Night, Curt Karish, Bobbie's night manager, lights a grill in front of the restaurant. After 90 minutes, the pork ribs and huli chicken are smoky and succulent. Early one afternoon a few summers ago, Curt was cooking chicken halves, that had been brined for two days with fresh limes and lemons, pineapple juice, salt and vermouth, when a familiar man sat at a nearby table wearing sunglasses and a baseball cap.

"This is the best brined chicken I've ever had," the lone stranger told Curt. "I have a couple of restaurants on the Mainland and I never really got into brining until recently. Now I'm brining everything, including prime rib."

Curt smiles as he recalls the memory.

"I took a closer look and it hit me," says Curt. "I said, 'Hey, are you...' The man took his hat off and said, 'Hey, I'm Bobby Flay.'"

Da Pakala Surf Pack #3 combo plate with teri chicken, chicken katsu and roast pork

G's JUICEBAR

9681 Kaumuali'i Hwy., Waimea
808-634-4112
www.Instagram.com/GsJuicebar
Juice, Smoothies and Açaí Bowls

"My passion for health didn't come from me always being healthy," says Garren Millare, owner of G's Juicebar and a 28-year-old Air Force veteran who was born and raised in Hanapēpē. "I used to eat canned food, corn beef hash and fast food when I was deployed in the desert in Qatar and Iraq."

While in the Air Force, Garren was diagnosed with Crohn's, an inflammatory disease than can be managed through diet. He was surfing the internet when he stumbled upon juicing as a method of healing. In 2011, he quit taking prescribed medication--which made him anemic, "foggy" and lost--and started juicing. He hasn't had a flare-up since.

"Juicing is great when you have Crohn's disease, because your small intestine is damaged and you can't absorb nutrients," explains Garren.

Inside his small shop, every inch of space is covered with colorful murals and signs that educate customers about the benefits of foods such as ginger, kale and carrots. A chalkboard menu features items like yerba mate, a tea made from rainforest tree leaves that are prized for strengthening the immune system.

Açaí Bowls are made with frozen bananas and açaí, a berry rich in antioxidants. They are topped with honey and house-made granola and come in flavors such as strawberry, coconut, raw cacao powder and nibs, natural peanut butter and dragon fruit.

They don't use dairy here, and smoothies are made with frozen bananas as a base. Hula Girl is a blend of strawberries, papaya and mango juice. Jah-G includes dates, natural peanut butter, house-made granola, cacao nibs and almond milk. Ironman is made with organic hemp protein powder, dates, kale, natural peanut butter, vanilla, cinnamon and almond milk.

All fresh juices contain ginger and include 20/20, a low-sugar blend made with carrots, apples, kale and lime. Michelangelo is made with pineapple, carrot, orange and lime juice. Donatello is made with beets, apples and lime.

"Being healthy has made an impact on my life," says Garren. "It would be a waste if I didn't help people with the knowledge I've gained. Life is about helping each other."

Garren Millare, Alisha Millare, Georgie Millare, Pukaua Kini at the colorful G's Juicebar

GRINDS CAFE

4469 Wai'alo Road, 'Ele'ele
808-335-6027
www.GrindsCafe.net
American and Hawaiian

Grinds offers more than 100 menu items including pizza, burgers, sandwiches, salads, fresh fish, pasta, and breakfast that's served all day long. In fact, you can get any menu item, any time of the day. Pastries, cookies and bread are baked fresh daily and available for take-out. They even serve a patty melt (one of my favorite type of burger), which is topped with grilled onions and Swiss cheese, and served on rye bread.

Everything is made from scratch including spice blends and sauces, so let them know if you have specific dietary concerns. Owners Christine and Kirk Marois also own Island Taco in Waimea and cater the sunset dinner cruise for Blue Dolphin Charters. Portion sizes are large at Grinds but the Mini Menu offers half-orders and children sizes. Sports fans will appreciate the two large flat screen televisions and a covered outdoor dining area that offers a view of the ocean.

SEA SALT & SEASONING

HANAPĒPĒ SEA SALT IS A CENTURIES-OLD TRADITION IN WHICH FAMILIES MAKE SEA SALT IN CLAY-LINED PONDS. THIS SALT CANNOT BE BOUGHT, BUT IS ONLY GIVEN AWAY OR TRADED AS WAS THE CUSTOM HUNDREDS OF YEARS AGO. TO BUY SEA SALT, CHECK OUT THE ALOHA SPICE COMPANY STORE. THE DELIGHTFUL SHOP IS PACKED WITH FOOD LOVER'S PARAPHERNALIA, AS WELL AS THEIR SEASONED BLENDS MADE WITH FINE-GRAINED SEA SALT. TRY MAKING A POPCORN SEASONING WITH EQUAL PARTS PELE'S FIRE AND KIAWE SMOKED GARLIC. IN SUMMER 2014, SALTY WAHINE GOURMET HAWAIIAN SEA SALTS OPENED A SHOP IN HANAPĒPĒ. THEIR BLENDS ARE MADE WITH COARSE-GRAINED SEA SALT. WE ESPECIALLY LIKE HOT LAVA WITH ROASTED GARLIC AND HAWAIIAN CHILI PEPPERS. MANGO JAVA, MADE WITH KAUA'I COFFEE, TENDERIZES STEAK WHILE ADDING FANTASTIC FLAVOR.

̓AFÉ & BAKERY

̄ Road, Hanapēpē

e.org/hanapepe-cafe-1
and American

It's early Friday evening as dozens of vendors prepare their stalls for Hanapēpē Art Night. Along the sidewalk, Midnight Bear Breads sets out loaves of warm bread made in Hanapēpē Café's kitchen. Next to them are pots of the café's soup, which are also sold every Wednesday during the Kaua'i Culinary Market at The Shops at Kukui'ula. (See page 141 for the full listing.)

Helen Lacono owns and operates Hanapēpē Café with her grandchildren and daughter Andrea Pisciotta Kaohi. High-backed chairs line a U-shaped bar with checkerboard tile. Nine tables are topped with votive candles and dressed with black tablecloths, silverware and paper napkins.

A small menu features three soups, three salads, seven entrées and six desserts. Baskets of fresh-baked focaccia and small pitchers of fruity olive oil are given to each guest. You can enjoy goblets of fresh-brewed tropical iced tea, or there's a $5 corking fee if you bring your own wine.

Bombas, a spicy purple sweet potato patty, is studded with whole shrimp and chunks of white fish. A side of Romesco sauce is made with fire-roasted red bell peppers and plenty of garlic. The dish is served with a salad consisting of local greens, carrots, cucumber and avocados, tossed with lemon honey Dijon vinaigrette.

"More food than plate. That's how we do it here," granddaughter Ku'ulei tells me while carrying a mountain of Eggplant and Spinach Lasagna to a nearby diner.

Pan-seared ono with lemon butter sauce is served with cucumber salad and dill yogurt dressing; black rice pilaf with celery and pecans; and tender green beans with thinly sliced carrots tossed in a spicy tomato sauce.

Lacono is the author of *Kaua'i Farmers' Market Soups*, which is available at her table every Wednesday during the Kaua'i Culinary Market at the Shops at Kukui'ula. The cookbook features 16 of her most popular soups, including Hungarian Mushroom and Pineapple Avocado Gazpacho Soup.

"Mom and I cook on Tuesdays for the Wednesday market and on Thursdays for Friday's dinners," Andrea says. "It's great because we're back there working, joking and laughing like we never have before."

Mango and lilikoi cobbler at the cafe

152

JAPANESE GRANDMA'S CAFE

3871 Hanapēpē Road., Hanapēpē
808-634-0101
www.japanesegrandma.com
Japanese and Sushi

When Japanese Grandma's Cafe opened in July 2016, it brought a touch of urban sophistication to Hanapēpē. The casual eatery serves traditional Japanese food made with high-quality ingredients in a clean, bright setting.

Before Owner Keiko Napier extensively renovated, the building was a USO club during World War II and starred in films such as *The Thornbirds* and *Flight of the Intruder*. Today, half the space is Blu Umi, a retail shop offering comfortable lady's fashion as well as handcrafted jewelry and art. The other half is a seven-table restaurant where Shinji Ueki, a Japanese master sushi chef, quietly works behind a counter.

You can order takeout, and eat in the large garden out back, or sit inside the air-conditioned cafe. An extensive sushi menu changes seasonally and fresh fish flown in from Oahu and Japan. The Combo Sushi Plate features an array of nigiri, including shrimp, halibut (cut to order from whole fish), ahi, kampachi, salmon and salmon roe, as well as a California roll and a fluffy cube of house-made tomago made with organic eggs.

Cold appetizers and small dishes include Kale Goma-Ae, an incredible kale salad with rich sesame dressing. Age-Mono (tempura) options are organic chicken, soft-shell crab, shrimp and locally grown vegetables.

Dinner entrees include Dinner Sets. These generous meals are served in covered bento boxes, and include miso soup, a garden salad, steamed rice, and three small bites of the chef's choice (ours included Kale Goma-Ae, Sunomono—crisp cucumber and wakame seaweed in a light dressing—and steamed asparagus with wasabi cream). Sets come with two of three main options: seared organic chicken or filet mignon drizzled with a light and semi-sweet teriyaki sauce, and mixed tempura.

"When deciding on menu items, I ask myself, 'If dad were alive, would this be okay with him?' says Keiko, who named the restaurant in memory of her grandmother. "He was a Japanese Master Chef who always said, 'To be worldly, you must understand food.'"

Note: Thomas Falchini, who cooked for Joël Robuchon, Tom Colicchio and Wolfgang Puck, is the chef de cuisine at Riviera Country Club in Pacific Palisades, CA. As of this printing, he is scheduled to lead Grandma's kitchen in Oct. 2016, to create non-Japanese meals and a new breakfast menu.

The Combo Sushi Platter is a perfect example of simple, clean sushi perfection

LITTLE FISH COFFEE

3900 Hanapēpē Rd., Hanapēpē
808-335-5000
www.facebook.com/LittleFishCoffee
Coffee Shop

BL $ 🩴 🍃 🌱VEGAN 🚫🌾 📶

Little Fish Coffee is tucked inside a yellow two-story building on Hanapēpē Road. There is limited seating inside, but there are tables with umbrellas in a quaint courtyard behind the restaurant. A lengthy drink menu includes espresso made with organic, Fair Trade coffee that's roasted weekly in Waimea. The staff was trained by an award-winning barista and uses an electric grinder that ensures that beans are the perfect consistency.

Hand brewed options include Moloaʻa Bay Coffee and 100 percent Kau coffee from Hawaiʻi Island. About a handful of espressos are flavored, but you can add house-made syrups such as cinnamon, hazelnut, caramel, almond and mint. The cardamom latte is well balanced and strong. The cardamon syrup cuts through but it's not overpowering, just great presence. I believe it's one of the best espressos on the island.

"We really take our time with the coffee and focus on making sure the quality is consistent," says owner Ethan Page.

Other beverages include tea, house-made chai and Italian sodas, such as the Sparkling Toddy, with cold-brew coffee, sparkling mineral water, house-made espresso syrup and a splash of cream. The drink is so sweet and decadent, it could be dessert.

Meals include salads, bagels and sandwiches. House-made hummus is spread over the Hippie Bagel; the Cobb Salad is dressed with a house-made vinaigrette and the Club-Zilla slathers house-made cilantro-pesto cream cheese on wholegrain bread.

The menu also includes smoothies and açai bowls, but I think the Poi Bowl is a delicious idea. A generous scoop of sweet poi is topped with fresh papaya, pineapple, blueberries, house-made granola, coconut cream and coconut shavings.

Cardamon latte is one of the best espressos we've had on Kauaʻi

"Poi is such a good food," explains Ethan. "It's hypoallergenic and healthy. We use Hanalei Poi Co., which is pasteurized, so it stays sweet."

Judy Page, Ethan's mom, bakes in the coffee shop's small kitchen. Her cinnamon rolls, pastries, banana bread, spiced vegan walnut bread, scones, cookies and brownies line the front counter.

"We try to use products that aren't shipped in," says Ethan. "They taste better, it's more affordable and there is less of a carbon footprint.

MCS GRILL

1-3529 Kaumuali'i Hwy., Hanapēpē
808-431-4645
www.MCSGrill.com
Hawaiian

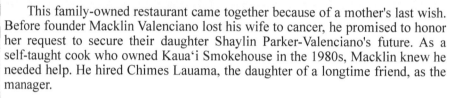

This family-owned restaurant came together because of a mother's last wish. Before founder Macklin Valenciano lost his wife to cancer, he promised to honor her request to secure their daughter Shaylin Parker-Valenciano's future. As a self-taught cook who owned Kaua'i Smokehouse in the 1980s, Macklin knew he needed help. He hired Chimes Lauama, the daughter of a longtime friend, as the manager.

Shaylin and Chimes are Native Hawaiians, born and raised on the Westside. Because Shaylin lost her mother to cancer and Chimes lost her 26-year-old brother to leukemia, they donate a portion of the restaurant's proceeds toward cancer research.

Macklin (M), Chimes (C) and Shaylin (S) offer local favorites as well as healthy dining options. You can order the popular Hawaiian Chili Peppa Fried Chicken with fried saimin and white rice, or the Vegetarian Trio, a filling appetizer of crispy tofu sushi rolls, Asian bulgur meatballs and curried brown rice with diced red bell peppers loaded into lettuce cups.

On Mondays, Macklin serves Oxtail Soup. A knobby bone loaded with succulent chunks of meat float in a house-made broth flavored with star anise. Tips of bamboo shoots are boiled twice and thinly sliced before shiitake mushrooms, cabbage and rice noodles are added.

Plate lunch comes with a choice of white or brown rice, tossed green salad, or mac and potato salad. Heads and tails are left on Kaua'i Shrimp Scampi. The Kekaha-raised shrimp are seared and fanned across a pile of fettuccine pasta that's flecked with mushrooms and drenched in cream. Thai Salad contains a generous portion of grilled sirloin, or optional pan-seared tofu, on a bed of greens, dressed with a tangy, house-made peanut sauce.

"We're trying to offer vegetarian and healthy options without taking away from the locals," says Shaylin. "You can still get your pūlehu steak and your cheeseburger and your healthy wife can have a grilled mahimahi salad with our homemade passion fruit vinaigrette!"

Amazing Oxtail Soup with bamboo
shoots and shiitake mushrooms

Midnight Bear Breads

3830 Hanapēpē Rd., Hanapēpē
808-346-4949
www.midnightbearbreads.com
Bakery

Inside Midnight Bear Breads, the smell of fresh baked bread fills the air and a row of golden pastries line a countertop, including tarts and bread pudding. If it's morning, fresh and buttery croissants have just come from the oven and their flakey insides are filled with lilikoʻi (passion fruit) and cream cheese; house-made marzipan; chocolate chips; or mozzarella, sun-dried tomato and fresh basil.

Owners Ursa Swift and Evan McAfee start their day at 2 a.m., shaping dough that was made the day before using organic flour and a five-year-old sourdough starter. Ursa pulls the dough from the cooler and shapes it into baguettes and loaves, then sets them to rise in baker's couche, or non-stick cloths. They rise until doubled in size, then Ursa scores the tops in curvy patterns.

These croisants may not be the typical shape, but their taste and texture are far beyond ordinary

The French Sourdough's texture is exquisite. A moist and springy interior is encased in a chewy, hard crust. Country Sourdough is made with whole wheat and rye flours, and the Multigrain includes nine types of whole grains.

Other flavors include rosemary and Hawaiian sea salt, olive ciabatta, sesame sourdough, caraway rye, roasted garlic and rosemary, pumpkin cranberry walnut, taro sourdough, breadfruit sourdough, Hawaiian sweet bread, cinnamon raisin swirl and Okinawan sweet potato rolls. Gluten-free options include focaccia with herbs and garlic olive oil, sandwich bread made with brown rice, and a round loaf with six types of seeds.

Evan makes hummus by simmering dried chickpeas and removing the skin as they cook. He says it's a traditional, labor-intensive step, but it makes the hummus silky smooth. He toasts whole sesame seeds then blends them into a house-made tahini with whole cumin seeds that are toasted before they're ground, and then he adds juice from local lemons. He also makes macadamia nut butter and, when it's in season, makes a chocolate version with cacao that was grown in Hanapēpē.

Midnight Bear Breads sells freshly made pizza every Friday night from 6 to 9 p.m., during Hanapēpē Art Night.

GLOSSARY

CRACK SEED

Chinese snack made of dried fruit combined with salt and/ or sugar. Flavors include rock salt plum, li hing mui, honey mango and licorice peach.

CHICKEN HEKKA

Many residents with roots in the plantation era would likely say this is the classic plantation dish. The stir-fried dish is typically made with chicken, but pork or beef can be used. The one-pot meal is usually made with bamboo shoots, vegetables, long rice, soy sauce, ginger and sugar.

CHICKEN KATSU

Japanese preparation of chicken cutlets coated in bread crumbs (panko), deep-fried and sliced into 1-inch strips. It's typically served on its own, with a side of steamed white rice and mac salad, or over saimin.

CHICKEN LONG RICE

A soupy mixture of chicken broth, long rice, shredded chicken and green onions.

FURIKAKE

Japanese condiment usually made of dried seaweed, bonito flakes, sesame seeds and salt, typically used to garnish steamed rice. It can also be sprinkled on baked or fried fish, raw fish salads, and popcorn or snack party mixes.

HALO HALO

Filipino frozen dessert made with shaved ice, fruit, sweet beans, jello or other sweets topped with custard or ice cream and evaporated or coconut milk.

HAMACHI

Hamachi is a Japanese amberjack fish, also known as buri. It comes from the belly of the fish, has a rich taste and texture, and is frequently used in sushi.

HE'E

Hawaiian name for octopus. Pronounced "heh eh." Japanese name is tako.

HAUPIA

Traditionally, this custard-like dessert was made with fresh coconut meat that was pounded and thickened with arrowroot. Today, coconut milk is blended with cornstarch, chilled until firm and cut into delicious cubes. Pronounced "how pee a."

'INAMONA

Hawaiian seasoning made from kukui nutmeat that has been roasted, ground and mixed with salt. This is a typical seasoning in poke.

KALBI

Korean barbecued beef short ribs marinated in a sweet soy and sesame mixture. Kalbi refers to grilled dishes in Korea.

KĀLUA PORK

Traditionally, whole pork was cooked in an underground oven called an imu along with vegetables such as sweet potatoes, taro and breadfruit. Today, most kālua pork is made in an oven with pork shoulder, liquid smoke and salt. Some commercial lū'aus use an imu and families have pits in their back yard where they also tuck in a pan of rice pudding. If you ever get a chance to try rice pudding cooked in an imu, take it!

KŪLOLO

A traditional dessert made with taro and coconuts. White or brown sugar is added to the thick mixture and cooked. My best description is a Hawaiian brownie that is sticky and slightly sweet. A special treat is kūlolo made with brown sugar and cooked in an imu.

LAULAU

Pork, chicken, fish or vegetables sprinkled with sea salt and wrapped in taro leaves, and steamed for up to eight hours. To prevent disintegration, the bundles are wrapped in inedible ti leaves; when cooked, the taro leaves resemble spinach.

LI HING MUI

In Chinese, "li hing" means traveling and "mui" means plum. The sour fruit, which is related to plum and apricot trees, is preserved in salt and flavored with sugar or licorice. Li hing mui can be purchased whole for a snack, or powdered and sprinkled on fresh fruit or rimmed in cocktails.

LOCO MOCO

Originating in Hilo, on the Big Island, loco moco is an iconic Hawaiian comfort food. Author Arnold Hiura describes it best in his book Kau Kau: Cuisine & Culture in the Hawaiian Islands: "You start with a generous bed of steaming-hot white rice. Add a homemade hamburger patty, fried so the juices are still dribbling out of it. Gently slide an egg onto the burger so its yolk (sunny-side-up or over-easy) does not break until you're ready to eat it. Cover the whole concoction with brown gravy. Break the yolk so that it oozes down into the hamburger juices and brown gravy. Together, the yolk and juices and gravy cascade down into the starchy depths of the rice, filling every nook and cranny and completing the exquisite symphony of flavors that is the joy of loco moco."

LOMILOMI SALMON

Lomilomi means, "to massage" in Hawaiian, and that's what happens when cubes of salted salmon, ice, tomatoes and onions are mixed by hand. Over the centuries, Hawaiians perfected the art of preserving fish with salt. When salmon became available from Pacific Northwest and Alaskan sailors, it was embraced by the Hawaiians and added to their culturally diverse list of ethnic foods.

LONG RICE

Cellophane or Chinese bean thread noodles.

LŪ'AU

Taro leaves slow-cooked in coconut milk.

MACARONI SALAD

There's no direct line that points to macaroni salad's ubiquitous presence in Hawai'i. Pasta, potatoes and mayonnaise have European roots and may have been introduced by Mainland chefs cooking in resort kitchens. Or, plantation managers of European descent may have asked their domestic help to prepare the cherished dish. Either way, today's mac salad is made with macaroni and mayonnaise; other ingredients are left to the cook. I've had it with taro, or combinations of potatoes, carrots, peas, eggs and onions.

MALASADAS

Balls of Portuguese sweet pastry dough (similar to donuts, only heavier), deep-fried and rolled in sugar, cinnamon or a combination of the two. When done right, as by Marlena in front of K-Mart, they are crisp and sugary on the outside and springy on the inside. The moist, dense, yet light crumb is punctuated with air pockets and they are an absolute delight to eat.

MANAPUA

Chinese steamed or baked buns filled with meat. Fillings include sweet Chinese barbecued or roasted pork (char siu), lup cheong (sweet, oily Chinese sausage), chicken or vegetables. Manapua derives from mea ono pua'a; "mea ono" for cake or pastry, and pua'a (pronounced "poo ah ah") for pork.

MISOYAKI

Butterfish is gorgeous in its simplicity. It's not a type of fish, but rather, a typical preparation here in Hawai'i, also known as misoyaki, which means "miso – grill" in Japanese. Any firm-fleshed fish will work in the marinade made with miso and soy sauce. When cooked, the fish has a light caramelized coating and sweet favor.

MOCHI

A glutinous rice cake made with pounded, cooked rice and various flavorings. Mochi is a traditional food for the Japanese New Year and can be stuffed with sweet fillings or wrapped around ice cream.

PIPIKAULA

Pipikaula, meaning "rope beef," is a type of beef jerky inspired by the plantation era. Hawaiian cowboys, called paniolo, would rub thin strips of beef with sea salt and cure them outdoors. Today, flavor variations include shoyu, chili pepper and garlic

PLATE LUNCH

That's not a typo. Hawaiian Pidgin English drops the "s" and turns plate lunches into plate lunch. Plate Lunch is an affordable meal that is prepared quickly. Typically, a scoop of steamed white rice and macaroni salad accompany a main entrée such as chicken katsu, beef stew, teriyaki chicken or beef, chili, kālua pork, garlic shrimp, or kalbi short ribs. Younger generations of restaurant owners now offer healthier options such as a fresh salad and steamed brown rice.

POI

Cooked taro corms that are ground and mixed with water. This is traditionally served with salty food such as kālua pork or lomilomi salmon and not meant to be eaten as a stand-alone.

POKE

Poke (pronounced "po kay") means to slice, cut crosswise into pieces, as fish or wood. The dish is a simple preparation of raw fish, Maui onions, seaweed (limu), Hawaiian sea salt and 'inamona. 'Ahi poke features glistening cubes of sweet, raw tuna. Tako poke includes slow-cooked and tender he'e (octopus). Edamame poke is made with soybean pods drenched in soy sauce and sesame oil.

PONZU

Ponzu is a citrus-based sauce, similar to vinaigrette, that pairs well with vegetables, seafood and meat. The sauce originates from Japan and includes seaweed, rice wine vinegar, bonito flakes and a citrus called yuzu. In Hawai'i, it is typically made with shoyu as well as fresh lemon and lime juices. It can be used as a marinade, as a condiment to dip sashimi, sushi, tempura, edamame, or egg rolls in, or as a salad dressing.

PŪPŪ

A term used in Hawai'i for appetizers. The term may have originated in 1934 at Don the Beachcomber restaurant. (Pronounced "poo poo.")

SAIMIN

A bowl of this noodle soup is like wrapping up in a fuzzy blanket on a blustery day. There are always curly strands of noodles (made from wheat and eggs) floating in a light dashi broth. But the cook can add scallions, crab cake, char siu, eggs and chicken katsu. Although saimin is unique to Hawai'i, the dish originated during the plantation era and the name comes from two Chinese words: sai (thin) and mein (noodle).

SHOYU

Japanese word for soy sauce.

SMOKE MEAT

Smoke meat (not smoked) is pork smoked over a wood fire. Hawai'i's wild pigs are a cross between domesticated Polynesian pigs that arrived with the first settlers and

Europeans boars introduced by Western sailors. Due to lack of refrigeration, plantation workers used smoking as a method of preserving pork after it was hunted.

SPAM MUSUBI

In the tradition of Japanese onigiri, steamed white rice is shaped into a rectangle and wrapped in nori. When SPAM was introduced to Hawai'i during World War II, it became immensely popular. Under war rations, the long-term storage, availability and affordability of SPAM inspired residents to stock their pantry with the salty pork product. Onigiri is a Japanese snack made of steamed, white rice wrapped in nori. In Japan it's typically stuffed with pickled plum known as ume; salted salmon; dried, fermented and smoked skipjack tuna; an edible kelp called kombu; or tarako, Alaskan pollock. It was only a matter of time before a Japanese plantation worker in Hawai'i slipped a thick slice of seared Spam onto a rectangle of white rice, brushed it with teriyaki sauce and wrapped it in nori. Today, the satisfying snack food is typically found under warming lights at gas stations and grocery stores.

TERIYAKI SAUCE

A blend of soy sauce, sugar, ginger and garlic. It's used on chicken, beef vegetables and fish. In fact, the Hanalei Dolphin's signature Teriyaki 'Ahi is the best teri fish I've ever had. (See listing on page 21 for details.)

WARABI

In Japan, fiddlehead ferns are called warabi; in Hawai'i they're called hō'i'o. Growing wild in Hawai'i, these green slender stalks with curly tops were foraged along with bamboo shoots. Today, they're typically blanched and made into a salad with tomatoes, Maui (sweet) onions, ginger, sesame oil and soy sauce topped with cubes of crispy pork belly or slices of smoked pork shoulder.

ABOUT TASTING KAUA'I

Tasting Kaua'i is dedicated to educating people about how to eat well on the Garden Island, from seed to table. Founders, Marta Lane, a Kaua'i-based food writer, and Daniel Lane, a freelance photographer, share insider's information on their blog as well as food tours and this restaurant guidebook. Blog topics include Kaua'i food news and food-related events, as well as recipes, local product and cookbook reviews, and where and when to find seasonal, exotic fruit. Food tours offer an authentic taste of the Garden Island and an opportunity to meet Kaua'i's exceptional food growers and makers. To find out what's happening with food on the island right now, you can follow Tasting Kaua'i on Twitter, Instagram and Facebook, visit our website at www.TastingKauai.com, or call toll-free 1-888-431-6660.

ABOUT THE AUTHOR

Marta Lane is originally from Colorado, where she was in the television industry for 25 years and worked as a video editor for Starz and the 2008 Country Music Awards. She has been a Kaua'i-based food writer since 2010. Marta's writing has been published in *Kaua'i MidWeek*, *Hana Hou!* magazine, *AAA Hawai'i* magazine, *Edible Hawaiian Islands* magazine, Hawaiian Airlines website, *HILuxury* magazine, Jazzercise.com, *HFM Foodservice* magazine, *Kaua'i* Magazine, The *Garden Island* newspaper, *Gourmet News* magazine and *Hawai'i Ag* magazine. In 2012 and 2013, Marta was the Farm Chairperson for the Garden Island Range & Food Festival and has been a Board Director for the Hawai'i Agrotourism Association since 2012. She is on the organizing committee for the Kaua'i Writers Festival. Marta sits on the board for the Kapa'a Business Association, which hosts the Coconut Festival every October, and organizes the Tasting Kaua'i Coconut Cook Off.

ABOUT THE PHOTOGRAPHER

Daniel Lane is a freelance photographer who specializes in capturing life on Kaua'i. His beautiful and sometimes quirky images are seen every week in *Kaua'i MidWeek*'s Poll, Pa'ina Page and Eye on Kaua'i photo spread. Daniel's client list includes Hawaiian Airlines, Kōloa Rum Company, Jim Beam, UPS, *Modern Luxury* magazine, *Bon Appétit* magazine, *Kaua'i Traveler* magazine, *HiLuxury* magazine, *Edible Hawaiian Islands* magazine, JO2 restaurant, Tiki Iniki restaurant,

Kaua'i Juice Co., Kaua'i Coffee, St. Regis Princeville Resort, Sheraton Kaua'i Resort, Kaua'i Marriott Resort, Aqua Kaua'i Beach Resort, Kaua'i Visitors Bureau and rock stars Timothy B. Schmit (of the Eagles) and Donavon Frankenreiter. He also contributes "Yum Shots" for his wife's articles and captures love and family in scenic portraits and weddings. His images can be seen at www.PonoPhoto.com.

Daniel and Marta met on the slopes of Copper Mountain, Colorado, in 1995. They have worked together since 1997 and have been married since 1999. The Lanes live in Kapa'a, Kaua'i, with their dog, Spike a Kaua'i Humane Society survivor. He's what's referred to in Hawai'i as a Poi Dog (an unknown blend of breeds). The vet is not sure, but thinks he may be a mix of Airedale and Whippet. We lost, Lucy, a tri-colored Cavalier King Charles Spaniel, in 2015. R.I.P. Bug, we miss you!

Spike playing at Glass Beach, Port Allen, Kaua'i

Mahalo Nui Loa